The Negative Thought Detox:

30 Days To Positivity

Bonnie L Greene

Published by Bonnie L Greene, 2023

THE NEGATIVE THOUGHT DETOX: 30 DAYS TO POSITIVITY

First edition. December 22, 2023.

Written by Bonnie L Greene

Published in USA

Dedication

To my husband, Gailon

I sincerely dedicate this book to you, my biggest champion. Your encouragement and support have been the source of my inspiration. I am grateful for your belief in me, even during my moments of self-doubt. Although this achievement is mine in name, it is truly ours in spirit.

With the utmost love and appreciation,

Bonnie

DISCLAIMER

The objective of this book, "The Negative Thought Detox: 30 Days to Positivity," is purely informative. This book's information is not intended to diagnose, treat, cure, or prevent any illness or condition. It is not medical, psychiatric, or other healthcare advice. The material in this book does not replace professional advice from certified health care specialists.

While the author has made every effort to ensure the accuracy and completeness of the information in this book, we do not accept and thus disclaim any liability to any party for any loss, damage, or disruption caused by errors, whether caused by negligence, accident, or any other cause.

Remember that you are responsible for your health. If you have any questions about a medical or psychiatric problem, always seek the advice of your healthcare professional.

INTRODUCTION

Have you ever had one of those days where you wake up, and the first thing that comes to mind is that one embarrassing thing you said three years ago? Or you've had occasions when you looked in the mirror, and your first thought was something negative about yourself. You are not alone. We've all been there, and it's why you're holding this book right now.

Let's begin with a simple, sometimes neglected fact: You are human. Despite flaws, humans have evolved into incredible problem solvers, inventors, creators, and thinkers. However, with that beautiful gift of thought comes the double-edged sword of negative thinking. While our ancestors found negative thoughts helpful for detecting danger (such as a prowling saber-toothed tiger), in today's modern society, this formerly useful attribute can sometimes be more of a burden than a gift.

But before we get into the detox, let's take a moment to acknowledge the immense influence our thoughts have over us. Consider this: Negative thinking, such as "I can't do this," can keep you from taking on a challenge, impede your personal growth, or even prevent you from embracing a life-changing opportunity. Consider how many similar thoughts pass through our minds in a single day, week, or year. Isn't it a staggering number? The cumulative effect of these beliefs is enormous, affecting our lives in ways we often don't realize until we step back and assess.

What's the good news? You can free yourself from this negative cycle. Your brain, as adaptive and plastic as it is, can learn, grow, and change. This concept, also known as neuroplasticity, is the basis for why a 30-day challenge can make a real difference in your life. We aim for a mental fitness regimen designed to break the bonds of negative thought patterns.

You might think, "30 days seems like a short timeframe." "Will it truly make a difference?" To that, consider this task to be a starting point. It is the initial push required to get things moving. Once those wheels begin to spin and you see the transformative power of positive thinking for yourself, you'll be more likely to stick with these practices in the long run. So, in some respects, these 30 days are just the beginning. The journey you're about to embark on isn't just about throwing on a good face and disregarding life's challenges. That would be both impractical and, to be honest, naive. Instead, I aim to provide you with the tools, insights, and exercises to sort through your thoughts, distinguish the beneficial from the detrimental, and create a mental environment where positivity can thrive. Consider it a mental spring cleaning. We'll sweep away the cobwebs of uncertainty and let in the fresh air of optimism.

It's not to claim the path will be easy. As with any detox, there may be days when you want to give up when old thought patterns seem too deep to change. But remember that every effort you make brings you one step closer to becoming a more positive, powerful version of yourself. So, if the path becomes difficult, consider why you started in the first place. Remember your mental picture of a better, more positive you and allow it to propel you forward.

You may be interested, if not suspicious, about what awaits you in the following chapters. That's fine; skepticism is healthy. But I'll ask you to embrace this challenge with an open heart and mind. Accept each day as an opportunity to learn and grow, confront negative thoughts, and replace them with empowering, uplifting ones.

IV

So, are you ready to embark on this transformative journey? To discover the practices that can declutter your mind and fill it with positivity, backed by ancient knowledge and current science? If you answered "yes" (or even a hesitant "I think so"), then let's get started. Prepare yourself to challenge, reshape, and elevate your mindset.

Because, my friend, you might be amazed at the difference in your reflection in the mirror in 30 days.

Here's to a happier, more positive you. Let the detox begin!

Table of Contents

Chapter

1

UNDERSTANDING NEGATIVE THOUGHTS

Origins of Negativity

Negativity can sometimes sneak up on us, like an unexpected rain cloud on a sunny day or an annoying pop-up during a video. Why do our minds sometimes drift toward negativity even when circumstances appear favorable? To comprehend this, we must travel back to when humans first discovered fire and the wheel. We may find the origins of our contemporary thought patterns during these defining moments of our evolution. Therefore, let's travel through time to comprehend this better.

The Evolutionary Point of View

Throughout human history, negativity has served as a survival mechanism. Consider our ancient ancestors; their world bears little resemblance to ours. Instead of busy towns and cutting-edge technology, they confronted deep forests, vast plains, and several predators lurking in the shadows. Saber-toothed tigers, rival tribes, and the unpredictability of nature were daily concerns. In such circumstances, a tendency toward the negative was not a philosophical question; it was a life-saving instinct. Being aware of potential hazards, skeptical of unusual berries, and wary of unfamiliar territory ensured another day of survival. This constant state of attention and precaution became ingrained in our DNA over time, establishing an inherent warning mechanism for potential dangers.

However, it was not only external threats that shaped this attitude. Social dynamics were also important. Cooperation was essential in early human communities. It was critical to be accepted and valued by one's tribe. It meant that negative comments or criticism from peers was more than just a hit to one's self-esteem; it also compromised one's status inside the group's safety. As a result, our brains evolved to be especially alert to negative cues, critiques, or possible conflicts, continually striving to correct and adapt for communal harmony.

Environmental Aspect

Let us now travel forward in time. While most of us no longer need to worry about wild animals or opposing tribes, our primal instincts persist. These appear in various ways now. A nasty social media comment, a critical remark from a coworker, or an unanticipated challenge can all activate the exact age-old protective mechanisms. Our brain intensifies these negative impulses to protect us, often overshadowing the wealth of happy events surrounding us.

Furthermore, with its constant influx of information, the modern world frequently bombards us with tragic, dramatic, or worrisome news. There's a cognitive rationale for this: disastrous news grabs people's attention. Our primitive brain, still looking for threats, latches onto these bits of information, reinforcing our negative biases even further.

Personal Experiences

While our ancestors' DNA and our environment still significantly influence how we think, we also cannot undervalue the influence of our own life experiences. Each of us has a memory bag that includes a mix of pleasant, unpleasant, and "I'd rather not think about it" recollections. But frequently, the painful experiences are the ones that leave the most scars.

Remember when you were in school, and you provided the wrong answer, and everyone laughed? How about that first job interview that went wrong? These experiences, particularly when they are traumatic, have a peculiar way of sticking with you. They serve as our reference points, our yardsticks for predicting future outcomes.

Why is it crucial to comprehend these origins? Because knowledge is power. Realizing that our negative thought patterns have logical explanations, whether they stem from evolutionary wiring, environmental influences, or personal experiences, can be highly liberating. It indicates that negativity is not intrinsic to our identity. It is an inherited, taught pattern. And what you've learned can be unlearned or, at minimum, managed.

Recognizing that you are not "a negative person" but rather someone influenced by various factors can help you change your attitude. It might be the first step toward understanding these beliefs without allowing them to define you. As you'll see in the following chapters, this acknowledgment is essential to your 30-day challenge.

But for now, let us enjoy our newfound understanding. Remember that you are not defective or flawed if your mind occasionally wanders down the unfavorable lane. You result from a complex web of human evolution, environment, and experiences. In the following chapters, we'll look more closely at how these negative thoughts emerge and, more importantly, how to deal with them.

But before we go any further, pat yourself on the back. Understanding is the first step toward transformation, and you have just taken it. We are moving forward!

The Science of Thinking Patterns: Exploring the Brain's Intricacies

We must take a scientific detour as we continue our research into negativity. Don't worry, I'll keep it light. Our understanding of the human mind has come a long way, and new advances in neuroscience provide essential insights into why our brains think the way they do. Our process of obtaining knowledge and understanding through experiences, senses, and thought has long been a topic of fascination. Philosophers once studied the secrets of the human mind, seeking answers from the stars and spirits. Our desire to comprehend our thinking patterns evolved from abstract theories to actual scientific research over time. As we dig deeper into the realm of negativity and its origins, we must travel through the complicated pathways of our brain, guided by the torchlight of modern science.

The study of the brain, known as neuroscience, is about more than just the gray matter within our skulls. It encompasses the universe of neurons firing electric impulses, the delicate dance of neurotransmitter chemicals, and the extensive networks connecting various brain regions, resulting in mental processes, memories, emotions, and actions. It's like mapping the universe, except we're charting brains and synapses instead of stars and galaxies.

Our understanding of the brain was historically limited. Ancient cultures believed the heart, not the brain, was the center of emotions and thinking. After a few millennia, the Enlightenment era saw the rise of the notion that separate brain areas were responsible for different functions. We began to view and understand the brain's activity in real-time by the twentieth century, thanks to instruments such as the electroencephalogram (EEG) and, later, MRI and fMRI studies.

Why do neuroscience advancements matter when discussing thought patterns? We understand how our thinking mechanisms work as we delve further into the complexities of our brain's structure and activities. Every emotion we experience, every memory we recall, and every decision we make involves the complicated web of connections within our brains.

How does our innate skepticism relate to the complex nature of our thinking methods?

Like all other living things, humans have an innate survival instinct. Being aware of prospective hazards was a matter of life and death in the early days of our species. A stir in the bushes could indicate a lurking predator, and the person who paid attention to that negative input survived to pass on their genes. This tendency toward negativity, or what psychologists call the "negativity bias," has become embedded in our DNA through many generations.

Our brain is not only the result of previous evolutionary factors. Whereas our ancestors encountered apparent dangers, today, we endure more abstract challenges such as financial stress, marital difficulty, and societal pressures. Our brains handle modern problems by adjusting, reorganizing neuronal connections, and developing new ways of processing information.

The concept of brain networks is crucial to understanding our thought patterns. Consider these mental motorways, with specific routes becoming more conspicuous with repeated use. If you've ever heard the expression "neurons that fire together, wire together," you can see how these networks form. Simply put, the more we participate in a particular thought pattern, whether positive or negative, the stronger those brain connections get.

As we move forward in this exploration, it is vital to comprehend the dynamic nature of our brains. Our brains are not static entities; they constantly evolve, adapt, and alter in response to our experiences, surroundings, and willpower. Neuroplasticity and epigenetics shed light on how our behaviors, attitudes, and environment can impact our genes and brain circuits.

In the following chapters, we shall explore these intricacies in greater depth. By examining the structure of our brain, the history of our thought behaviors, and the remarkable adaptability of the mind, we can gain a deeper understanding of our thought processes. Suppose you wish to identify the source of your pessimism or cultivate a more optimistic outlook. In that case, this voyage will provide valuable and uplifting insights.

The Asymmetry of Perception: How the Brain Processes Negative vs. Positive Information

Our minds are like supercomputers, processing millions of bits of information daily. The flicker of light, the faintest aroma flowing from a bakery, and the momentary touch of a loved one all contribute to the constant flow of our consciousness. Our brain interprets negative and positive information differently, giving negative impulses more weight. But have you ever wondered why, out of all the information we receive, the negative often stands out like a sore thumb? Let's solve this riddle collectively.

Consider yourself at a gathering. The lights are dim, the music is pulsating, laughter is in the air, and you feel fantastic in your meticulously selected attire. You've been soaking in compliments all evening, but then, as you're about to leave, someone remarks that your shoes look "a bit odd." Suddenly, you can't stop thinking about it. The dozens of compliments fade into obscurity, and the solitary negative comment becomes the focal point. Does this sound familiar? The intriguing asymmetry of your perception is now before you.

Understanding the asymmetry of perception and the inclination to focus on the negative allows individuals to confront problematic thought patterns while seeking solutions that encourage a more balanced perspective.

The Reputable Negativity Bias: The Brain's Warning Label

The phenomena you just witnessed at the imaginary party is known to psychologists as the 'Negativity Bias.' Negativity bias is the most notable characteristic of this asymmetry. It is the belief that negative experiences or information influences our psychological state more than neutral or positive experiences. Our brains are like watchful watchdogs, constantly looking for anything that could endanger our safety. This bias is not a recent flaw in our systems; it is a profoundly ingrained mechanism that serves an essential purpose.

Several millennia ago, life was very different for our ancestors. The rustling of leaves could indicate the presence of a predator nearby. A misstep or missed cue might spell the difference between life and death. In such a situation, the brain will prioritize survival over the pursuit of pleasure. There are different repercussions for ignoring potential dangers and enjoyable opportunities, such as eating ripe fruit.

Inside the Brain: The Neuroscience of Emotions

We've been handed a rare ticket to the brain's emotional theater thanks to technological miracles, notably the introduction of functional MRI scans. The results of these scans are nothing short of amazing.

When exposed to potentially dangerous stimuli, certain areas of our brains light up like fireworks. The amygdala, our emotional processing center, is the main character in this show. It's the brain's drama queen. When it detects negative emotions, it lights up, causing rapid reactions ranging from heightened vigilance to an adrenaline rush that prepares us for action.

Positive emotions, on the other hand, take a more scenic trip. While they activate pleasure areas in the brain, such as the ventral striatum, the effect is often quieter and softer. They are the compassionate souls who make sure we have fun but may take a back seat when danger approaches.

Modern Implications: A Protective Mechanism Turned Potential Adversary

In today's world, saber-toothed tigers no longer pursue us, and our everyday threats are more about meeting deadlines and dealing with societal pressures. However, our ever-vigilant brain continues to run on outdated software. A rude remark made by a coworker is dealt with almost as quickly as an ancestral threat. This results in modern-day issues such as persistent stress, worry, and a tendency to dwell on the bad.

Though this predisposition safeguarded generations before us, it is now critical to understand when our negative bias is overreacting. We must remind ourselves to take a breather, step back, and reassess conditions. While being vigilant to risks is beneficial, being on high alert can harm our mental health.

By understanding the balance between positivity and negativity in our brains, we equip ourselves with valuable knowledge. We can build a more balanced, comprehensive perspective of life by becoming aware of our intrinsic prejudices. It's not to say that we ignore bad feelings; instead, we give equal, if not greater, weight to the more positive emotions, relishing moments of joy, thankfulness, and happiness. It's like updating the brain's software to ensure it's tuned in to the intricacies of our modern world, making life's journey more vibrant and satisfying.

Neuroplasticity: The Brain's Extraordinary Resilience and Ability to Modify Thoughts

People used to think of the brain as an old-school computer system; set it up once, and you're stuck with it. There are no vast updates, no dramatic enhancements, simply the same old program running day after day. For a long time, the brightest minds and researchers maintained this notion. However, a significant finding altered the narrative, as with all revolutionary breakthroughs in thinking. Then, neuroplasticity was a discovery that completely changed the script, redefining our understanding.

What Exactly Is It?

Neuroplasticity, also known as brain plasticity or neural plasticity, is a broad phrase that encompasses an essential idea: the brain's astonishing ability to change and adapt throughout a person's life. It's about substantial changes, not tiny adjustments, in which brain connections can be established, re-routed, or severed based on various internal and external variables. In other words, our brains are like dynamic artworks constantly altering and perfecting themselves.

The Forces Behind Neuroplastic Change

Learning and Experience

Whenever we learn a new skill, whether a musical instrument, a language, or even juggling, our brain works constantly. Neurons, the brain's primary cells, are highly active, forming new bridges known as synaptic connections. The more we practice and immerse ourselves in the learning process, the stronger these bridges get, resulting in the skill or knowledge to embed deeper into our brain network.

Environmental Factors

The phrase 'product of our surroundings' carries more weight than we might assume. Our settings, whether they are our homes, employment, or social circles, have a significant impact on our brain landscapes. Chronic stress, for example, can alter brain regions related to memory and emotion. On the other hand, supportive, stimulating circumstances can boost brain growth and strengthen positive pathways.

Brain Injuries

It's incredible how our brains adapt when damaged. When there is a brain injury, the brain's ability to change, also known as neuroplasticity, aids healing. Non-damaged areas of the brain may take over tasks from the affected area. It allows critical brain activities to continue even after impairment.

Thought Patterns

Consider the brain an extensive, complicated network of routes. A path (or thought) becomes more defined and apparent when followed. Consistently entertaining pessimistic thoughts can develop prominent brain pathways for pessimism. However, there is a silver lining; traveling good and constructive routes frequently enhances them, underlining their importance in our brain network.

Neuroplasticity's Potential Implications

Neuroplasticity is a light of hope, not merely a scientific phrase. It teaches us that our past does not determine our future and that change is possible.

Understanding neuroplasticity gives us power. If you find yourself in harmful thought patterns, you are not bound to stay caught in that neurological rut. You can carve out new, healthier paths with intentional effort, perseverance, and sometimes guidance. This guidance could include practicing mindfulness, seeking therapy interventions, or seeing the world more optimistically.

Using Neuroplasticity to Promote Personal Development

Recognizing our brain's flexibility is more than a fascinating fact; it's an invitation. It invites us to keep learning, connect with new places and experiences, and intentionally direct our thoughts toward happiness and growth. We can increase our neural health, well-being, and life satisfaction by actively participating in situations that challenge and stimulate our brains.

Neuroplasticity emphasizes a fundamental truth about human existence: change is not only conceivable but also deeply rooted in our nature. We can harness this inherent potential with determination, awareness, and a dash of optimism, steering our brains and, by extension, our lives down paths of enrichment, positivity, and holistic well-being.

Identifying Negative Thought Traps: Common Cognitive Distortions ~ Sneaky Mind Saboteurs

Let us embark on an exciting excursion deep within our imaginations. Our brains are amazing, but they are a little, well, dramatic at times. The stories they spin need to be grounded. These excessive or irrational thought patterns are known as cognitive distortions in psychology. Consider them to be pesky bugs in our mental program.

Let's take a deep breath and dissect some of the most notorious offenders:

Catastrophizing

Suppose your significant other fails to complete a task, the immediate thought is, *"I'm consistently disappointed and my needs are probably unimportant. "It's an indication that our relationship is hopeless."* That's an illustration of catastrophizing. It occurs when a small mistake escalates into a severe interpersonal issue. Rather than seeing it as a one-time slip-up or a small error that can be talked about and fixed, the mind makes assumptions about the whole status and future of the relationship, transforming a straightforward misplaced task into proof of a seriously problematic relationship.

Overgeneralization

Occurs when your brain magnifies a single experience and applies it to all situations. If you make a mistake during a presentation, you may think, "I always ruin things." "I can't seem to get anything right." It's like assuming that if it rains one day, it will rain every day.

Filtering

Your brain is wearing some seriously colored glasses in this situation. It amplifies the negative while filtering out the positive. Have you received nine compliments and one bit of constructive criticism? A filtering brain concentrates entirely on negative feedback, overshadowing all positive feedback.

"Should" Statements

Have you ever thought to yourself, "I should be more successful by now" or "They shouldn't behave like that"? Join the club of "should" statements. They create false expectations and can be a tremendous downer.

Personalization and Blame

You either take on too much responsibility (e.g., "It's all my fault our team didn't win.") or take on too little accountability, or shift the blame to someone else, completely absolving yourself.

The first step toward mental clarity is recognizing these cognitive errors. By noticing them, you become a more conscious observer of your thoughts, less influenced by their dramatic stories, and more grounded.

The Self-Fulfilling Prophecy: When Your Brain Plays Fortune Teller

Now it's time for some mysticism! So, you'd think with a phrase like 'self-fulfilling prophecy; No, it doesn't involve crystal balls or tarot cards, but it does include predicting the future.

Let's dissect it. A self-fulfilling prophecy is a forecast that comes true just because the person believes it. Doesn't it sound strange? It's when your mind creates a feedback loop: Belief = Behavior = Belief Confirmation.

Assume you're apprehensive about a social function because you believe you're awkward in social settings. So, you go, but keep quiet and to yourself. People then avoid you, which "confirms" your perception that you are socially awkward. But here's the catch: You're not naturally awkward; your belief in that idea has caused you to act withdrawn, resulting in less contact.

Here are two strategies to help you get off this mental merry-go-round:

As with cognitive distortions, understanding when you're creating a self-fulfilling prophecy is critical. It's all about catching your brain off guard when forming these ideas.

1. Challenge the Belief

Call it into question. "Is this belief based on solid evidence or just a hunch?" People frequently build their beliefs on assumptions rather than facts.

Instead of thinking, "I'm awkward," how about, "I'm a good listener, and not everyone has to be the life of the party." Finding a more balanced viewpoint is the goal of reframing.

2. Change Your Behavior Actively

The self-fulfilling prophecy is remarkable because it demonstrates the power of our brain. Our beliefs can create our realities. However, with knowledge and deliberate action, we may ensure our thoughts develop our mental well-being for the better, resulting in positive, rewarding outcomes.

Recognizing these negative thought traps is like discovering a map in a maze. It's about navigating our thoughts' intricate hallways with extraordinary elegance, understanding, and less drama. You'll have the tools to return your brain to the balanced center the next time it spins tales of disaster or pretends to be a fortune teller. Here's to brighter, more precise, and more sensible thinking!

Chapter

2

THE PSYCHOLOGY BEHIND NEGATIVITY

The Connection Between Thought Patterns and Emotions

The human brain, a biological miracle, is a complicated network of interconnected neurons, each capable of processing massive amounts of information. The symbiotic relationship between our thoughts and emotions is essential to our knowledge of ourselves and our interactions with the world. Both have a significant impact on our perceptions, actions and overall well-being.

Consider your thoughts a continuous stream in which words and images ebb and flow, sometimes fluidly and sometimes tumultuously. These thoughts, whether conscious or subconscious, lay the groundwork for our emotional reactions. Each idea is like throwing a stone into a still pond, causing ripples of connected emotions to spread outwards.

Now, Consider the importance of memories. Dwelling on a prior mistake or misstep can immediately elicit feelings of regret, embarrassment, or melancholy. These emotions aren't just passive reactions; they have a significant impact on our future decisions, making us more cautious or discouraging us from taking similar risks in the future. When feelings of fear or dread overtake us, our thoughts frequently take a darker turn. They spiral, focusing on future uncertainty, exaggerating risks, and recalling past traumas or setbacks, all of which contribute to our anxiety.

Our thoughts and feelings have an unbreakable connection, and there's actual science that supports it. When we have a particular thought about something, our brain releases neurotransmitters, and hormones. These chemicals behave like messengers, translating our thoughts into our emotions. Our brain has a complicated mechanism in which thoughts generate signals, which convert into the feelings we know.

Dopamine, also known as the 'feel good' neurotransmitter, is linked to pleasure, reward, and motivation. When we engage in a favorite activity or achieve a goal, the release of dopamine helps us feel satisfied, rewarding positive behaviors. Similarly, serotonin, which governs mood, hunger, and sleep, is essential for emotional equilibrium. Serotonin shortage is associated with negative thoughts and emotions of sadness and can contribute to diseases such as depression. Another neurotransmitter, norepinephrine, functions as a stress hormone and a neurotransmitter. It is necessary for alertness, emotions, sleeping, dreaming, and learning. It can elicit the "fight or flight" reaction, but in moderation, it may also enhance mood.

Cortisol and adrenaline, on the other hand, serve as our body's alert system. These hormones are released during moments of stress or perceived threat and prepare us to respond. They are lifesaving in the short term, enhancing our perceptions and speeding our reactions. However, constant stimulation of these hormones results in persistent negative thoughts or chronic stressors that contribute to emotions of discomfort, anxiety, or downright fear. The extended presence of such hormones can even be harmful to our physical health, affecting heart health, immunity, and various other aspects of our lives.

Understanding the profound link between thought patterns and emotions, as well as the biological mechanisms that underpin them, is more than just academic. It gives us the awareness to be more intentional in guiding our thoughts, understanding the emotional responses they generate, and potentially using this information to improve our mental health. Recognizing these patterns allows you to make proactive efforts toward creating a more balanced emotional landscape, one in which thoughts work to uplift rather than undermine.

When we want to break destructive behaviors, we start with the intimate relationship between thoughts and emotions. Let's see how this relates to the larger concept of detoxing negativity.

Awareness is Key

Understanding the sources and consequences of negativity is critical before addressing and detoxing it. Understanding how thoughts can evoke specific emotional responses allows us to spot harmful patterns as they emerge, making detoxification more effective and targeted.

Biochemical Reinforcement

Recognizing that our thought patterns aren't just abstract and have genuine, physical, biochemical effects adds urgency to the process. Detoxing negativity has tangible benefits for our brain chemistry and our physiological health, in addition to making us feel better mentally.

Empowerment through Knowledge

Realizing we can change the tune by understanding the delicate dance between our thoughts and feelings. If our negative thoughts consistently cause worry, anxiety, or unhappiness, we can elicit different, more positive emotional responses by changing or questioning these thoughts.

Breaking the Cycle

The feedback loop, in which unfavorable thoughts encourage negative feelings and vice versa, can create a negative self-perpetuating cycle. The first step towards ending the pattern is to recognize it. By detoxifying negativity, one aims to break the habit and replace it with a more positive, reinforcing cycle.

Dealing with Chronic Stressors

Understanding the long-term impacts of cortisol and adrenaline in the body highlights the importance of detoxing negativity. Chronic stress and continuous negative thinking can be harmful to one's health. Addressing and detoxifying these noxious behaviors contributes to improved physical health.

Essentially, this guide emphasizes eliminating negative factors from our lives. It's incredible how our seemingly insignificant thoughts can have such a tremendous impact on our emotions and general state of mind. When viewed in this light, we must actively strive to create a more pleasant mental environment.

Understanding Common Emotions: Fear ~ Anger ~ Sadness ~ Guilt

Isn't life a rollercoaster? We're all going through these wild ups and downs, sometimes feeling on top of the world, sometimes not. And four biggies dominate this emotional journey: fear, anger, sadness, and guilt. Let's talk about each of them.

Fear

Do you remember that scene in a scary movie where the tense music begins to play, and you know something terrible is about to happen? That rush, that racing heart, that's terror in action. Fear served as our early warning mechanism, according to evolutionary theory. Fear kept us alive while hiding in caves and escaping saber-toothed tigers. It told us to 'RUN!' or 'HIDE!' when we were in danger.

Fast forward to the present day, the circumstances that cause fear have also evolved. Sure, we still experience it when faced with physical threats, but it's also there when faced with modern challenges like nervousness about speaking in public or the fear of peer criticism. The difficulty is when dread takes up residence and becomes a frequent guest. Constant, unmanaged fear is not only unpleasant; it can lead to anxiety disorders.

Anger

Have you ever experienced driving down the road, humming to your favorite music, when suddenly, bam! Some vehicle speeds by, cutting you off. Or you're sitting on your couch and come across a news story that makes your blood boil? Your heart rate accelerates, and that familiar, blistering sensation of rage begins to simmer within you. Anger has historically played an essential part in our survival toolbox, alerting us to prospective threats and preparing us for conflicts. It was a vital emotion, motivating us to defend our resources, protect our loved ones, or face trouble immediately.

Anger triggers have altered significantly in recent years. These days, violations of one's boundaries are triggers, sentiments of being underappreciated or overlooked, or even a colleague taking credit for your work rather than defending one's territory or resources. Anger, however, isn't just intense and destructive. It's also that overwhelming pressure that causes us to exclaim, "Enough!" It inspires our desire for justice, piques our interest in causes, and can unite communities to effect change.

But here's the point, and it's critical. If you allow anger to simmer for too long, it will explode like a pressure cooker. Without the proper understanding or management, this powerful emotion can cascade, resulting in rash judgments and broken relationships. It can paint our words with harsh tones or, worse, start tearing at our physical health.

Heart problems, high blood pressure, you name it, and unrestrained rage have a long list of consequences.

Sadness

Ah, sadness, the emotion that has inspired innumerable songs, films, and late-night conversations. Do you feel down after a breakup? That is sadness. Do you have the blues as a result of a lost opportunity? Again, sadness. It's a widely felt emotion, something that binds all of us together in our shared experience of being human. It's normal, sometimes even necessary, like rain after a long period of sunshine. But what's indeed striking about sadness is how it typically leads to contemplation and reflection.

It provides a little break from our hectic life, allowing us to refocus. We delve deeply into our feelings and experiences during these reflective times. We think back on the choices we've made in the past, analyze the significant issues facing life, and look forward to our goals and dreams.

Like persistent rain can cause massive floods, prolonged sadness may indicate more serious underlying problems. Although it's normal to experience sadness following significant life events, such as the death of a loved one or a difficult transition, it's important to distinguish between sentiments that pass quickly and ones that linger and meddle with our daily activities. When melancholy appears unending, consumes one's life, and interferes with day-to-day functioning, it may be an early symptom of disorders such as depression.

Therefore, while it is acceptable to periodically allow feelings of melancholy to wash over us, which can provide us with a much-needed shift in perspective or a deeper connection with others, it is equally as important to know when it is time to reach out to others and perhaps even seek the assistance of a trained expert. After all, every feeling, including melancholy, contributes a chapter to the epic story that is our life, serving as a teacher, a guide, and a facilitator of our personal growth.

Guilt

Have you ever taken an extended lunch break and found that the rest of the day, you were uncomfortable because of it? Or you missed a friend's important event and started avoiding their calls, that constant feeling of guilt making every ringtone sound even more accusing. Recall the occasion when you unintentionally revealed someone's secret and hoped the other person wouldn't find out for the remainder of the week. Join me as we unravel the tangled web of guilt.

Consider guilt to be an internal alarm. When we do something that goes against our principles or what others expect, it's like a subtle reminder from our conscience. The brain tells you to "think twice before doing that again." It functions as a tool to encourage behaviors that keep individuals close. The emotion of guilt enables us to reflect on our behavior and make constructive adjustments.

In everyday life, guilt acts as a moral compass, directing us toward actions and decisions consistent with our values and beliefs. Whether it's the shame of snapping at a loved one or ignoring a vital promise, this emotion forces us to admit our mistakes, enabling reconciliation and personal progress. We are motivated to evaluate and modify our behaviors when confronted with feelings of guilt. However, like with many things in life, balance is critical. A pinch of guilt can be beneficial, urging us to make amends, apologize, and strive for personal growth. It motivates sincere regrets, deeds of kindness, and introspective decisions. It encourages us to volunteer, assist others, and reach out when someone is in need. Guilt is a beautiful ally in these situations, motivating us to be the best version of ourselves.

However, if unrestrained, guilt can transform from a constructive advisor to an oppressive tyrant. When we're continually swaddled in shame, feeling guilty about the most minor mistakes, alarm bells should go off. Chronic guilt can lead to a warped sense of self in which inadequacy overwhelms us, and we regard ourselves as constant screw-ups. It can cast lengthy, gloomy shadows over our self-esteem, coloring our reality with sorrow and self-doubt. Such sentiments can accumulate over time, resulting in tension, anxiety, and even despair.

Furthermore, it is critical to distinguish between authentic and fake guilt. Actual guilt is the result of genuine wrongdoing, whereas unauthentic guilt is the result of unrealistic self-expectations or external pressures. It's the guilt that makes you feel guilty for not going to that party while fatigued or for not taking on that extra project despite having an overflowing plate. Recognizing and dealing with such misdirected guilt is critical for maintaining mental health.

Understanding your emotions is an essential step toward dealing with negativity. Fear, anger, sadness, and guilt all have profound evolutionary roots, playing diverse roles in influencing your choices and reactions to the world around you. You have a better chance of dealing with these emotions proactively if you can identify their source and understand what drives them.

Knowledge becomes your instrument, enabling you to navigate your feelings carefully rather than impulsively. This proactive attitude not only keeps emotions from overwhelming you but also allows you to channel them in ways that benefit your personal development. By doing so, you turn potential stressors into opportunities, strengthening your resilience and improving your general well-being.

The Cycle of Stress and Negativity: How Negative Thinking is Influenced by Stress and Vice Versa

Life has its high-octane moments: deadlines to fulfill, unanticipated bills to pay, and a growing pile of laundry. As much as we wish to avoid them, these stressors are an unavoidable part of our lives. But have you ever noticed that under stressed times, everything appears a bit gloomier? Let's dive into the intricate connection between stress and negative thinking and observe how they frequently overlap.

Cortisol, a beneficial hormone, is at the center of this connection. Consider cortisol to be the body's inherent alarm clock. It's like that vivacious friend who says, "Hey, something's up!" whenever there's a hint of trouble. While it's helpful in actual emergencies (such as fleeing a hungry lion in our ancestors' days), it's less valuable when it's blasting because you can't locate your keys in the morning. Cortisol, while necessary in short bursts, becomes an issue when always present. Chronic cortisol spikes can cause our brain to become hyper-focused on the bad.

So, why does our brain tend to focus on the negative when we are stressed? Our ancestors could be the culprit. Back in the day, survival often rested on anticipating what could go wrong. A rustling in the bushes? It's best to imagine it's a predator rather than a calm wind. To survive, our ancestors had to prepare for the worst constantly. Nowadays, though, worrying about a missed email or a misplaced text message seems excessive. But, hey, old habits die hard, and we're still wired to be on the lookout for problems, no matter how minor.

The feedback loop between stress and negativity is comparable to that between a loud crowd at a sporting event and their team's performance. The more the crowd cheers, the more hyped (or anxious) the team becomes. Similarly, as we grow more stressed, our negative thoughts become louder. It can be a complex cycle to break because one reinforces the other. A minor hiccup can quickly snowball into a full-fledged avalanche of tension and unhappiness.

While getting stuck in mental loops is a serious worry, the consequences of this cycle extend beyond our minds. Our bodies take the brunt of the damage as well. Chronic stress and its accomplice, persistent negative thinking, can establish the framework for a variety of health problems. We're talking about a weaker immune system (hello, frequent colds!), elevated blood pressure, and sudden aches. Mentally, it lays the groundwork for diseases such as anxiety, depression, and even burnout.

With continuous messages, full inboxes, and the pressure to keep up, today's fast-paced society fuels an already raging fire. We are inundated with information designed to pique our interest by exploiting our worries or insecurities, and our brains are constantly fed stressors, which makes it even more difficult to break free from the grip of negative thinking.

The relationship between stress and negativity is complex, firmly ingrained in our evolutionary history, and exacerbated by our current lifestyles. Recognizing and managing this cycle is the first step. While it may appear difficult at times, with the appropriate methods, we can convert this pattern into something more balanced. Our brains are unique, and with some mindfulness and modifications, we can turn them into allies rather than foes.

Breaking the Cycle: Relaxation and Mindfulness Exercises

Deep Breathing

When stressed, your body produces cortisol, the "stress hormone" I previously described. Slow, deep breaths activate the body's natural relaxation response, lowering cortisol levels, which lessens jitters and increases feelings of comfort. While some cortisol is fine (and natural), too much for too long can be depressing.

Deep breathing is more than just taking a big gulp of air. It's a mindful technique that requires you to breathe deeply into your diaphragm, filling your lungs and then gently exhaling. Consider it like blowing air into a balloon: steady, consistent, and controlled.

Here's a Guide:

Locate a comfortable spot: This could be your favorite chair, a nice corner, or simply parking yourself on the ground. Check that you are comfortable and that your posture allows for full lung expansion.

Close your eyes: It aids in focusing on the breath and reduces distractions.

Inhale via the nose: Count to four as you breathe in, allowing the air to enter your lungs deeply.

Hold and exhale: Hold your breath for four counts, then exhale through your mouth for another four counts.

Rinse and repeat: After a few times, you'll experience the magic!

Advantages of Deep Breathing:

Stressbuster: As previously said, deep breathing lowers cortisol levels, making it a very efficient approach to de-stress. So, the next time you feel like a kettle about to whistle, try it.

Improves Circulation: More oxygen signifies improved circulation, which means you'll be more awake and sharper!

Improves Mental Clarity: A clean mind can face problems better, make decisions faster, and generally feel lighter. Deep breathing is analogous to restarting a faulty computer.

A Natural Painkiller: You read that correctly. Breathing deeply releases endorphins, your body's natural happy pills. They aid in relieving pain and the induction of emotions of contentment or euphoria.

Aids Digestion: Deep breathing increases oxygen delivery to all body parts, including our digestive system, allowing it to perform more efficiently.

Sleep Well: Having difficulties falling asleep? Deep breathing can help calm your body and mind, allowing you to sleep more profoundly and soundly.

Deep breathing has real, measurable advantages. A few minutes a day can put you on the road to a healthier, more relaxed you. Take a deep breath and delve into the calm underneath the storm the next time life feels like a whirlwind.

PMR (Progressive Muscle Relaxation)

Relieving physical tension involves tensing and relaxing distinct muscle groups in the body. It is like putting your body through a workout at the gym, except that you are working out the tension knots and kinks that accumulate in your muscles rather than lifting weights.

You begin by tensing a specific muscle group (such as your fists or toes) for a few seconds, then letting go and enjoying that lovely, sweet relief. You work your way up (or down) your body, from your toes to your brow, tightening and releasing each part. What is the benefit of this? When we are worried, our muscles tend to tighten without our knowledge. Have you ever had a crick in your neck or a heavy feeling in your shoulders after a long day at work? That is your body's response to stress. PMR enables your muscles to relax and rejuvenate.

Benefits of PMR

Mind-Body Connection: Developing awareness is another goal of PMR, in addition to making your muscles feel supple and relaxed. You may become more aware of your body's cues and gain an initial awareness of how stress affects it by purposefully tensing and then relaxing.

Reduction of Muscle Tension: Obviously, this one! After a hard day, PMR can help ease those bothersome aches and pains by actively relaxing your muscles.

Better Sleep: Do you toss and turn at night? PMR can assist with it. You're laying the groundwork for a better night's sleep by unwinding your body before turning in.

Mood Enhancer: Your mood usually follows physical well-being. You may also experience an emotional weight release when you let go of bodily stress.

Mental Distraction: Paying attention to tensing and relaxing will help you focus on anything other than the hundred things on your to-do list or those annoying negative thoughts.

Tips:

Find a quiet place: PMR works best in a peaceful environment. Find your Zen area, whether a quiet room in your home or an isolated corner in a park.

Comfort is essential: Sit or lie down in a comfortable position. Take a comfy pillow or blanket with you!

Take your time: Avoid rushing. Spend time working on each muscle group, concentrating on the tension and then the relaxation.

Regular practice: As with any skill, the more you practice it, the better you will get. Aim to practice PMR regularly to gain full advantages.

Think of PMR as your body's stress-relief toolset. It's easy to do, effective, and all you need is, well, you! So, the next time tension has you wound up tighter than a drum, try PMR. Your muscles (as well as your mind) will be grateful!

Mindfulness Exercises with Guided Imagery

Guided imagery taps into this remarkable talent that we all possess, transporting us away from our current stressors and into more peaceful regions. Visualizing a pleasant scene or situation could induce emotions of relaxation and reduce stress levels. While it is a clever approach, you've most likely used it without realizing it.

Remember those childhood fantasies when you imagined yourself as a wizard wielding powerful spells or a dragon rider soaring over mystical skies? Or how about being aboard a giant pirate ship in pursuit of hidden treasures?

That was the core of guided visualization in your young mind. As adults, we can consciously channel our imaginative abilities, transforming them into beautiful tools for relaxing and healing.

Exactly What is Guided Imagery?

Guided imagery is a focused technique that uses all five senses to create cheerful and relaxing scenarios in our minds. It's not just about "seeing" a beautiful beach; it's also about feeling the sun on your skin, hearing the soothing waves, tasting the salty air, and smelling the sea. Consider yourself to be holding a ripe, juicy orange. Even if you don't have the fruit in your hands, your imagination can readily conjure up its tangy aroma, the feel of its rough skin, and even its pleasant flavor. That is the capability of our minds to simulate experiences. All these aspects contribute to the imagined scenario feeling vivid and real.

Guided imagery, at its core, taps into this fundamental ability. It isn't just restricted to the visual senses. It is about using all our senses, including touch, taste, sound, smell, and sight. The method creates an immersive atmosphere by calling each sensation, transforming a basic image into a multi-dimensional experience.

You may wonder how "thinking" about anything may help us feel truly comfortable. Everything is connected to the brain. When using guided imagery, your brain doesn't know the difference between a vividly imagined encounter and a genuine one. As a result, the same brain pathways are stimulated. Simply, if you vividly visualize yourself relaxing by a tranquil lakeside, your brain may react as if you were there. Similarly, picturing yourself biting into a sour lemon may make your mouth water. In its marvelous complexity, your brain treats the unreal and the real with remarkably comparable responses.

Imagining the Ideal Scenario

The flexibility of guided visualization is what makes it so appealing. Whether you prefer the mountains, the beach, or the peaceful corners of a bustling city, guided imagery can be adapted to your specific needs. While one person may find serenity envisioning a sunlit forest glade with birds singing in the treetops, another may find comfort in a cozy room with a crackling fireplace and the rich aroma of brewing coffee.

To get the most out of the exercise, you must create scenarios that are personally meaningful to you. The more personalized and detailed your visualization, the more powerful the encounter. Consider places or settings historically providing calm or joy, then expand on them. What time is it? How is the weather? Are there any distinct sounds or smells? The mosaic becomes deeper as additional layers are added.

While the purpose is usually relaxation or happy visualization, guided imagery can also address and manage negative emotions. An individual may be encouraged to picture confronting a source of fear or anxiety under the supervision of a qualified practitioner. It can be a step toward overcoming or managing that challenge.

Including Guided Imagery in Your Routine

Starting with guided imagery can be as simple as scheduling a few quiet moments throughout your day. You could start by listening to guided meditation recordings accessible online or through various meditation applications. As you become more comfortable with the routine, you may find it more straightforward to navigate yourself through your creative visions that are ideally fitted to your interests and needs.

Why Does it Work?

In many ways, the brain can't distinguish between a vividly imagined and an authentic experience. Consider the last time you had a vivid dream; your heart may have raced, and you may have even sweated, all while safely snuggled in bed. Similarly, when you immerse yourself in a peaceful visualization through guided imagery, your body reacts as if you're truly experiencing it. Your heartbeat may become steadier, your muscles may relax, and your daily stresses may lessen.

Visualization, from a neurological standpoint, can activate the parasympathetic nervous system. This biological system encourages relaxation in our bodies. When we immerse ourselves in a relaxing visualization, we signal to our bodies to reduce tension and enter a healing and relaxation state.

Guided Imagery for Beginners: A Basic Method

Find a calm spot: While you can technically practice guided imagery anywhere, a calm, distraction-free environment is preferable. Dimming the lights can also create the desired atmosphere.

Close your eyes: This helps to block off exterior stimuli, allowing you to better focus on your inner world.

Deep breathing: To quiet your initial thoughts, begin with a few minutes of deep breathing.

Choose a scenario: Consider a place or setting that you find entirely tranquil. It might be a memory, or something completely made up.

Activate your senses: It's important to remember that it's not only about sight. What are you hearing? Smell? Taste? Feel? The more senses you engage, the more vivid and immersive the experience becomes.

Stay in the moment: If your mind wanders (and it will), gently direct it back to your chosen images.

It is optional to set aside specific times for guided visualization. However, it is highly recommended. Once you've mastered the method, you can use it in everyday stressful situations. Do you get nervous before a meeting? Consider a soothing waterfall, listen to its sound, and feel its mist. Are you stuck in traffic? Consider a peaceful country road.

Guided imagery is a dynamic and diverse therapy that provides substantial pathways for healing and personal development in addition to relaxation. Create genuine, concrete changes in your emotions, body, and overall well-being by creating vivid, sensory-rich experiences in your brain. The key, as with any skill, is practice and patience.

Professional Assistance

Although individuals can practice guided imagery independently, having trained professionals guide you through these visualizations often enhances the experience by bringing to light subtleties that may be overlooked otherwise. Professionals can be especially effective if you are struggling with substantial challenges or trauma.

Body Scan

The word "body scan" may sound like something from a Star Trek episode, but it's an ancient meditation practice. It is a meditation practice in which attention is carried successively around various parts of the body, recording feelings and encouraging mindfulness and relaxation. It's about being present, tuned in, and taking a mental journey through your body. Long before meditation applications and modern health retreats popularized the body scan, it originated in ancient rituals. The body scan is a component of mindfulness meditation, a centuries-old practice, particularly within the Buddhist lineage. The essence of the body scan is straightforward; it involves focusing your attention on your body, part by part. Imagine your mind as a low-beam flashlight, and with each breath, you illuminate a new region of your body, studying any feelings you meet without judgment.

Why Do a Body Scan?

"Why should I pay such close attention to my body?" you might question. I feel a pain in my back, and my feet are a bit cold. "What's the big deal?" The actual value of a body scan extends beyond physical awareness. By paying more attention to our body, we increase our sense of the present moment, noticing subtle sensations that are frequently overlooked in the everyday buzz of life. This increased awareness strengthens our connection to ourselves and our surroundings.

Furthermore, the body scan has a subtle way of encouraging relaxation. It's not uncommon to discover areas of stress you didn't even know existed as you move from the tips of your toes to the crown of your head. Simply observing them (without attempting to change anything) causes these places to relax and release themselves on their own.

A Step-by-Step Guide to Body Scanning

Begin by locating a comfortable, quiet place where you will not be disturbed. While many people like to perform this while lying down, you can do it while sitting. Just make sure your spine is straight and that you're comfortable. A straight spine aids in maintaining good bodily alignment. The remainder of the body follows the spine's alignment. This position helps to reduce pressure on muscles, tendons, and ligaments, allowing for an extended and more comfortable meditation period. The spine is thought to be the central route for the flow of energy or "Prana" (in yogic words) or "Chi/Qi" (in Chinese traditions) in many spiritual practices, particularly those found in Eastern philosophies. A straight spine allows this energy to flow continuously from the base of the spine to the top of the skull.

Close your eyes, take a few deep breaths, and begin with the tips of your toes. What are your thoughts? Perhaps it's the gentle brush of your socks, the weight of a blanket, or a tingling sensation. Don't pass judgment; observe.

Move slowly: Begin with your toes and gradually work up to your ankles, legs, etc. Take the time with every section to truly connect and experience that specific part.

Engage all senses: While the primary focus is feelings, don't be surprised if other senses want to come along for the ride. Temperatures, textures, and even minor sounds, such as fabric rustling, may be noticed.

Distractions are allowed: Your thoughts will wander. It's entirely natural. When you realize you're thinking about supper or reminiscing about that 90s sitcom, gently bring your focus back to your body, just where you left off.

Finishing touches: Once you've gone from head to toe (or toe to head if you're feeling a little rebellious), relax and feel your entire body. Breathing deeply, savoring the sense of serenity and connection.

Benefits

Numerous studies have indicated that body scanning can have various advantages. Aside from the immediate feelings of relaxation and centering, frequent practice can help with chronic pain, sleep, and emotional resiliency. We can often recognize stress or tension earlier and proactively address it if we know our body's sensations.

Furthermore, the body scan can be an effective method for increasing self-compassion. In a culture where we are frequently encouraged to be critical of our bodies, this technique provides a safe space by enabling us to view our bodies with kindness and curiosity rather than condemnation.

Mindful Meditation

Mindful meditation is a technique based on being objectively present in the moment. It helps to notice and disconnect from negative thought patterns, viewing them as fleeting clouds rather than fixed realities.

Mindful meditation is a well-known practice that entails more than just sitting quietly; it's a technique designed to ground you, binding your thoughts to the present moment. Let's explore deeper into the benefits of this soul-calming technique.

The practice of mindful meditation is traced back to ancient

Buddhist traditions, where monks and spiritual practitioners used it to achieve enlightenment and self-awareness. However, limiting its significance to ancient times is only partially correct. The essence of this practice has traveled far beyond its Buddhist origins over millennia, finding resonance and adaptation everywhere, transcending cultural and religious barriers.

The technique has been modified and reimagined to match the requirements and ideologies of diverse cultures and societies, from the venerable halls of Tibetan monasteries to the fashionable urban yoga studios of New York.

Why is there such universal appeal, you may wonder? In our current society, characterized by constant digital stimulation and information overload, mindful meditation appears as a haven. Imagine navigating a loud, crowded, and ever-changing digital concert and then discovering a serene nook where the timeless tones of a vintage instrument provide an oasis of tranquility. That is the solace mindful meditation offers in the middle of our modern lives, making it an essential tool for anyone seeking balance, clarity, and a deeper connection to themselves.

Mindfulness is all about being fully and completely present. It's not about blocking out all thoughts or attaining some mystical blank slate. It is instead about observing your ideas, feelings, and sensations without attempting to change them. It's like sitting on a riverbank and watching the water go by. The water represents your ideas, and you, the observer, are apart from them.

Tips For Getting Started:

Set the Scene: Locate a peaceful area. It doesn't have to be a beautiful Zen Garden; it may be your bedroom, a corner of your living room, or even a park bench. The goal is to have as few distractions as possible. Dim lighting and a comfortable seat can enhance the atmosphere. The idea is to maintain a relaxed yet attentive posture, whether in the conventional lotus position, on a chair with your feet flat on the floor, or any other position that feels good.

The Breath: This is the point at which the magic begins. Focus on your breathing and close your eyes. Feel the airflow into and out of your nostrils or mouth. Take note of how your chest and abdomen rise and fall. The breath is an anchor, keeping you anchored in the present moment.

Observing Thoughts: Now comes the tricky part. Thoughts will dance around as you meditate. It could be a grocery list, a recollection from five years ago, or concerns about a meeting tomorrow. The idea is to acknowledge these thoughts without judgment, not to push them away. Consider them to be passing across the sky like birds.

Bringing It Back: It's inevitable that your thoughts may stray. When you find yourself becoming caught up in a thought or mood, gently bring your attention back to your breath. It's not about chastising yourself for being distracted but recognizing the detour and returning to the present.

What's the point?

Mindful meditation is more than a fad. There is a growing number of studies demonstrating its benefits; here are a few:

Stress Reduction: By concentrating on the present, you are less likely to dwell on past regrets or future concerns, lowering cortisol levels.

Emotional Awareness: Recognizing and categorizing your emotions helps to reduce their intensity and make them more bearable.

Improved Concentration: Regular meditation can improve concentration, making activities appear less demanding and more feasible.

Sleep Soundly: Mindfulness activities have been found in studies to improve better sleep. Consider it a natural lullaby for the mind.

Enhanced Resilience: By noticing thoughts without getting caught up, you can cultivate a more resilient mindset, less susceptible to being affected by every passing feeling.

In essence, mindful meditation is about developing a deeper connection with yourself and understanding the ebbs and flows of your mind. It is not so much a matter of eradicating negative thoughts as identifying them and choosing not to get caught up in the storm. It provides a sanctuary of serenity in a world saturated with constant noise, even for a few minutes daily. And, let's be honest, who couldn't use a bit more peace?

The Link Between Mindful Meditation and the Detoxification of Negative Thoughts

Even if the practice of mindfulness does not explicitly aim to eradicate negative thinking, it is intrinsically linked to the detoxification of negative thoughts. The following is a breakdown of how they are related:

Understanding vs. Eliminating

It is critical to understand that mindful meditation is not about removing or concealing negative thoughts. Instead, it is about comprehending, recognizing, and watching them. It allows us to see these thoughts for what they are temporary and fleeting mental creations rather than concrete facts about ourselves or our reality.

Detachment

As we notice our thoughts without judgment during meditation, we begin to detach from them. Recognizing signifies that we do not become entangled in the narratives that our minds construct. Rather than spiraling into anxiousness after a thought such as, "I'm not good enough," one can analyze their ideas and think, "Ah, there's that thought again," without spiraling farther into negativity.

Breaking the Cycle

Negative thoughts frequently lead to negative emotions, leading to more negative thoughts, creating a feedback cycle. Mindful meditation aids in breaking the loop. We can avoid this chain reaction of impact by examining our thoughts without becoming consumed by them. Essentially, we disrupt the negative feedback loop.

Developing a Neutral Response

With the consistent practice of meditation, we can learn to react calmly to adverse events or thoughts. We can avoid acting on impulse and instead think through our options. It does not imply that we are indifferent; alternatively, it allows us to respond in a controlled manner.

Enhancing Positive Thoughts

Rather than focusing only on thinking positively, mindfulness is about being in the moment and embracing our emotions as they arise. We stop battling against negative thoughts by practicing this acceptance.

When we stop focusing solely on pushing away negative thoughts, our minds are free to develop positive ones. Consider it like a garden; the flowers have a higher chance of blooming if we don't overcrowd them with weeds.

Reduced Stress

Negative thoughts are frequently exacerbated by stress. Stress has been demonstrated to be reduced by mindful meditation, and this can lessen the occurrence and potency of negative thought patterns. Reducing stress also improves judgment and cognitive clarity, which further minimizes negativity.

Increased self-awareness

Mindful meditation helps you to become more conscious of your thought patterns and emotional triggers. Because of your increased self-awareness, you will eventually be able to recognize when negative thoughts are starting and handle them more effectively.

Mindfulness teaches us that everything changes, even our thoughts. It's one of the most important lessons we can learn. By internalizing this idea, we are less likely to hold on to or be shaped by our negative thoughts because we realize that they are just fleeting moments throughout our expansive mental terrain.

While mindful meditation does not try to "delete" unpleasant thoughts, it does empower the mind, allowing people to handle adversity with more ease, clarity, and understanding. In essence, this helps detoxify persistent, harmful thought patterns. Understanding the psychology of negativity gives us priceless insights into our actions, attitudes, and emotions. We can disrupt the negativity cycle by realizing the interconnectedness of thought patterns, feelings, and stress. Developing awareness and actively seeking relaxation and mindfulness practices not only combats negativity but also fosters a balanced, holistic well-being.

Chapter 3

THE 30-DAY CHALLENGE FRAMEWORK

Preparing for Success

Participating in a 30-day challenge is an admirable activity demonstrating dedication to personal growth and self-improvement. While gratifying, the procedure needs a disciplined approach based on careful planning. As with any major project, success in a 30-day challenge is dependent not just on milestones met but also on the meticulous planning that precedes the challenge.

It is critical to understand the rationale behind a 30-day framework from the start. This duration, which spans a whole month, was carefully chosen due to its inherent benefits.

Attainability: For most people, a month-long commitment is a reasonable goal. It's a length that allows for quantifiable development without stretching so far that goals become hazy or unclear. You can more precisely picture your journey with a fixed start and end date.

Manageability: A 30-day timeframe is a manageable time frame for creating short-term goals. The time frame is long enough to develop and maintain new habits but short enough without feeling overwhelmed. It ensures that you maintain a consistent level of participation and dedication.

One of the critical goals of a 30-day challenge is to create the groundwork for long-term habits. This duration, which is both short and brief, provides a sustainable pace. During this time, you can firmly insert practices, boosting the possibility that these habits will last beyond the assignment's completion.

Consider the importance of preparation for your challenge as establishing the foundation for a structure. The success of your endeavor is based on the foundations you lay, just as a magnificent construction depends on a solid foundation for its stability and durability. A good start ensures you are not left on shaky ground and exposed to unforeseen obstacles and outside pressures.

While enthusiasm is a tremendous motivator and the initial driving force behind success, it is only one piece of the puzzle. Passion can ignite the fire that propels people on their quest. However, in the absence of a clear plan, excitement might fade or, in some situations, misdirect efforts. It is vital to have a clearly defined road map to guide the journey.

Effective Planning: Multiple Stages

Setting Goals

Clearly outline what you intend to accomplish by the conclusion of the 30 days. It could be something practical, like reducing weight, or something more abstract, like finding inner peace. To be more explicit, this could be minimizing the frequency of negative thoughts or creating a more positive outlook. The most important thing is to have a clear vision of what you are seeking to accomplish.

Mental Preparation

Preparing oneself is essential. It entails envisioning success, comprehending potential risks, and mentally mapping out overcoming obstacles.

Some Potential Risks May Include:

Overload and Burnout: Taking on too much too soon can result in feelings of overload. Excess can lead to burnout, which discourages people from continuing the challenge or trying again in the future.

Unrealistic Expectations: Setting overly ambitious objectives or expecting dramatic changes quickly might lead to disappointment if those goals are not achieved.

Relapse or Reversion: If no plan is in place to maintain the new changes beyond 30 days, there is a chance of relapsing to old habits or behaviors.

Feedback Mechanisms

Plan on how you will track your success. Regular check-ins, whether daily or weekly, can provide significant insights into your journey, allowing you to adjust as needed.

Setting Specific Goals: The Compass for Your 30-Day Journey

A well-defined intention is at the center of any meaningful journey. Consider this: would you go on a month-long road trip without knowing where you're going? Sure, a day or two of impromptu driving might be thrilling, but a month-long trip without a plan? That will undoubtedly result in you wandering or, even more, getting stuck in a tedious loop. As a result, in the context of your 30-day challenge, establishing a specific goal is like entering your desired destination into a navigation system, giving the purpose and direction of your effort.

Let's dig a little deeper. What does it mean to "set an intention"? It's about getting to the bottom of the 'why' of your problem. Consider the inner motivations that drive you. Is it a desire to learn a new talent that you've been putting off? Is it a quest for better mental health, or are you attempting to create resilience by pushing yourself? Your intent is the steady light you can rely on, especially when the path becomes shrouded with uncertainty or setbacks cast shadows of doubt. When motivation wanes, it is your clear purpose that will illuminate your way and keep you focused on your final goal.

However, creating intentions entails more than just selecting a goal. It's about understanding the essence of the plan. Get into specifics; instead of saying, "I want to get in shape," say, "I want to incorporate 20 minutes of physical activity into my daily routine to improve my stamina and overall well-being." The more specific and individualized your desire, the more tangible and attainable it appears.

It's also worth noting that while clarity of purpose is essential, the journey is about something other than laser-focused accuracy. There is beauty in evolution and in allowing oneself to adapt as one progresses. Your 30-day challenge will surely provide unexpected difficulties and learning curves. Some days, you may struggle with emotions of inadequacy or the urge to jump ship entirely. Instead of criticizing yourself in those circumstances, consider what you want to accomplish. Allow it to serve as a reminder of the bigger picture. Every day you endure, no matter how small the step you take, you get closer to your goal.

Even though goals are a guide, they are not a strict way to measure. Embrace the journey with understanding and compassion. Remember that it's not a race. Setting a clear goal isn't about how fast you're making progress; it's about making sure your efforts are going in the right direction. It means ensuring that every step, no matter how small, is a step forward. Celebrate the small wins, learn from the setbacks, and let your goal be the constant that helps you get back on track.

Goals provide an overall sense of direction. Allow your plan to serve as both a compass and an anchor as you embark on this 30-day adventure.

Tools: Your 30-Day Expedition Arsenal

Are you ready to go on a journey of learning and challenge? The road ahead is exhilarating, but it is not without its twists and turns. Not to worry! With the correct tools, you can confront almost any challenge.

Journal: Your Reflective Companion

A journal is more than a diary; it's your challenge partner. Consider it a secure place to scribble down daily experiences, accomplishments (big or small), and even challenges. It gives you an outlook by showing you how far you've come, especially on days when you feel like you're trapped in quicksand. Furthermore, it is a wonderful tool for reflecting on developments and growth.

Your Mighty Quill

While it may seem obvious, having a dedicated pen for this journey makes it more memorable. Consider it the Excalibur of your 30-day knight's tale. Choose a pen that excites you to write and commemorate your adventure, whether it's a fountain pen, a gel pen, or even a quill (hey, no judgments here).

Supported Community ~ Your Cheer Brigade

It is often remarked, "Together, we achieve more." It's especially true while undertaking a 30-day challenge. Creating or joining a supportive group can give you the wind beneath your wings. It could be a close-knit group of friends, understanding family members, or an energetic online group brought together by a common struggle. The key is to have people who understand, sympathize, and motivate.

They'll celebrate your accomplishments, provide a sympathetic ear at difficult times, and yell words of encouragement from the sidelines on days when the journey feels too rigorous. They are, in essence, the optimistic energy, the collective force that magnifies your desire, the tribe that assures you that you are not traveling alone.

Days 1-10: Awareness and Acknowledgment

During these first ten days, the main goal is to become acutely aware of your thought patterns, especially the negative ones. It is not about immediate change; instead, it is about recognizing them, understanding their origins, and acknowledging their presence without becoming engulfed by them. The goal is to help you notice and accept these thoughts without passing judgment while using various techniques.

Daily Exercises to Identify Negative Thoughts as They Emerge

1. The Mindfulness Bell: A Deep Dive into Self-awareness

In an age of constant connectivity and endless to-do lists, our minds are always racing, switching between tasks, chores, and fleeting thoughts. This continuous mental noise can sometimes make it hard to hear our thoughts and figure out what they are about. A simple tool like the Mindfulness Bell can help us get back in touch with our thoughts in a profound way.

It's critical to recognize the significance of self-awareness before getting into the details of the Mindfulness Bell. Our daily behaviors, attitudes, and decisions result from unconscious thinking. These beliefs, over time, can impact our actions, habits, relationships, and overall well-being. Being more aware of our thoughts allows us to change our lives for the better while also providing us with clarity.

What is the Mindfulness Bell?

The Mindfulness Bell concept is simple yet profound. It uses a soft, periodic chime or alert throughout the day, drawing on mindfulness practices. Every time this bell rings, it serves as a reminder to return to the present moment. But what exactly does this entail? The aim is to pause whenever the bell sounds, to stop whatever you're doing mentally or physically, and check in with yourself. Take a deep breath and ask yourself, "What was I thinking?" "How am I feeling right now?" It's a moment of reflection that allows us to tune into our internal dialogue. After identifying the thought, your next step is to comprehend its nature.

Thoughts are classified as:

A} Constructive or Destructive

Was the thought uplifting, providing answers, or inspiring you? Was it beating you down, pointing out imperfections without offering progress, or simply instilling anxiety in you?

B} Factual or Speculative

Did the thought have a basis, something you are sure of? Or was it something that came from your fears, presumptions, or fantasy?

Making such decisions does not involve judging oneself. Instead, it is about gaining insight into the nature of your thinking patterns.

Why is this regular check-in necessary? "Is this frequent introspection vital?" The answer is found in the cumulative effect. While a single negative or speculative thought may not have a substantial impact on your mood or decisions, a sequence of these thoughts over the day might lead to increased tension, worry, or even erroneous behavior. By periodically scrutinizing our thoughts, we avoid being swept away by a torrent of unrecognized negativity or speculation.

This strategy, when used daily, can drastically alter one's way of thinking in a variety of ways:

Increased Self-awareness

The more you practice, the more you will increase your ability to identify subtle differences in your thinking.

Decreased Reactivity

Being in tune with your thoughts reduces the likelihood of reacting impulsively or based on uncontrolled emotions.

Improved Mental Hygiene

The first step in altering harmful habits is recognizing them. Once you've determined which thoughts are damaging or speculative, you may address their underlying causes or replace them with more constructive ideas.

Adapting the Bell to Your Specific Needs

While the essential concept remains unchanged, the frequency and nature of the bell can be changed. Some people prefer a chime every hour, while others prefer more frequent reminders. The sound should be soothing and non-jarring, such as a mellow chime, birdsong, or even a gentle gong. It should be a sound that inspires meditation rather than one that shocks.

Incorporating the Mindfulness Bell into one's routine may appear to be a minor intervention, yet the effects can be profound. In a society where we're becoming increasingly detached from ourselves, tools like these serve as vital bridges, reconnecting us to our core and reminding us of our deepest thoughts and sentiments. As you work through this exercise, you'll likely discover its simplicity is its most powerful feature, providing a clear road to increased self-awareness and mental well-being.

2. The Thought Tally: A Method for Quantifying Negative Thoughts

Quantification operates as a magnifying glass in many facets of life, bringing previously unseen patterns into great focus. Quantification can be an illuminating, if not transformational, tool for studying our mental processes. Why is it necessary to measure something as abstract and transitory as thoughts, particularly unpleasant ones? The answer lies in increased self-awareness, better mental health, and personal growth.

The Quantification Effect

Humans are intrinsically inclined to under or overestimate certain behaviors or tendencies, mainly when they occur subconsciously. For example, if you were to guess how many times you checked your phone in a day, your estimation could be way off the mark. Similarly, without a disciplined process such as tallying, one may be blind to the sheer volume of negative thoughts that take root in the mind regularly.

We provide tangible evidence of an intangible process by quantifying it. This tangibility has the potential to be game-changing. When you see your negative thoughts represented physically through tallies, you understand their prevalence and significance.

The method itself is simple, yet its simplicity is what makes it so effective. Prepare a little notebook or a particular page on your smart device. You make a small tally mark every time you catch a negative thought, whether self-doubt, judgment, pessimism, or any other shade of negativity. Returning to these markings as the hours pass can often lead to startling revelations. It's a wake-up call for many. The sheer number of tallies can reveal how much mental space these unwelcome thoughts occupy.

Benefits That Go Beyond Numbers

While seeing a sheet full of tallies may cause surprise or even alarm, the exercise's primary goal is not to instill guilt or self-judgment. Instead, its functions are numerous:

Increased Self-awareness: Recognizing the existence of a problem is critical before tackling it. This exercise sharpens your mental antennae, making you more sensitive to negative frequencies.

Pattern Recognition: As you routinely log these tallies, you may notice trends. Your negative thoughts may be more intense at various times of the day, or specific triggers or situations exacerbate them. Recognizing these patterns is the first step toward devising solutions to combat or manage them.

Grounding and Presence: Pausing to tally promotes a moment of mindfulness. It brings you back to the present moment, providing a little break from the flurry of thoughts.

Data Empowerment: Knowledge is power. When you have hard statistics on the frequency of your negative thoughts, you can create realistic goals and track your progress over time.

As the days develop into weeks and you stick with this activity, the emphasis shifts away from drastically decreasing the number of tally marks, though that may be a good bonus. The actual essence of this technique is to develop a keen awareness of your mental environment.

In the long term, this awareness can be the foundation for more significant interventions, such as cognitive behavioral therapy, meditation, or any other form of mindfulness practice. After all, you can't fix something you don't recognize.

Despite its simplicity, the tally system is essential in improving mental health. It highlights the often-hidden corners of our minds by transforming our negative ideas into something we can see and count. This technique promotes not just self-awareness but also greater understanding and personal development.

3. Reflective Journaling

Reflective journaling is a contemplative and introspective technique in which people record their thoughts, feelings, experiences, and reactions to certain events or situations. The emphasis is on going deeper, assessing the event, contemplating its consequences, and gaining insights and lessons from it. The primary purpose of reflective journaling is to promote greater understanding and learning. It's a means to connect with and make meaning of one's positive and unpleasant experiences. In contrast to a daily diary or notebook, which may record events or tasks, a reflective journal goes a step further. It could include reactions to triggers, thoughts about specific experiences, feelings about human encounters, or reflections on difficulties encountered.

But, aside from its appeal, how can it function as a powerful tool for negativity detoxing?

We can uncover negative patterns lying beneath the surface by documenting our experiences. It could be a reoccurring uncertainty, a nagging concern, or a series of depressing thoughts. We're halfway to confronting and changing these habits if we recognize them.

Second, the act of writing itself can be cleansing. It's not only about recording emotions but also about processing them. When bad feelings or thoughts weigh on us, writing them down can help to lighten their load. It's like unloading heavy luggage.

Finally, reflective writing serves as a constant means of letting go when it comes to detoxing from negativity. Consider it a brain cleanse, in which negative thoughts are wiped away to create a space for an entirely new point of view. This space not only allows for the recognition of negative thoughts but also a deeper understanding of them, working through their sources and eventually replacing them with more positive and constructive insights.

Reflective journaling prompts to help get you started:

Prompt 1. "Today, the most recurring negative thought I had was..." Explain your thoughts. When did it occur? Can you think of any triggers? Investigate its roots and determine whether it is founded on facts or assumptions.

Prompt 2. "A situation today where I felt out of place or uncomfortable was..." Consider your current state of uneasiness. What aspects of the surroundings or interaction influenced this feeling? Were specific people or themes to blame? Documenting these experiences may uncover recurring triggers or circumstances that test your comfort, allowing you to manage them more effectively in the future.

Prompt 3. "Today, I found myself avoiding..." Investigate this avoidance habit. Was it a task, a person, a memory, or an argument? What feelings did the prospect of confronting it elicit in you? Identifying and writing about these avoidance habits may reveal underlying anxieties or insecurities, allowing you to face them head-on.

Prompt 4. "An emotion I didn't expect to feel today was..." Dive into this unexpected feeling. What triggered it? What impact did it have on your conduct or thoughts for the rest of the day?

Prompt 5. "A memory from the past that resurfaced today was..." Investigate the emergence of this memory. What prompted its reappearance? What effect does it have on you right now? You can acquire insights into unresolved emotions or comprehend the patterns and events that shape who you are today by revisiting and exploring these memories.

Prompt 6. "One interaction today that left a lasting impression on me was..." Consider the specifics of this conversation. What stood out to you about it? How did it affect your emotions, thoughts, or behaviors for the rest of the day? Analyzing these primary contacts can reveal insights into your interpersonal dynamics, as well as potential areas for growth or appreciation.

Prompt 7. "Today, I felt most at peace when..." Consider this peaceful moment. What were the events or environments that produced this serenity? How can such moments be recreated or extended in the future? You can actively seek and incorporate these pockets of tranquility into your daily life by identifying them.

Prompt 8. "Something I heard, read, or saw today that resonated with me was..." Investigate why it hit a nerve. Does it support or contradict your personal beliefs? How does it relate to or differ from your current living situation? Recognizing what connects with you might help you better understand your core values and views.

Prompt 9. "If I could offer my morning self, one piece of advice based on how today unfolded, it would be..." Consider the events of the day and consider what advice or forewarning may have helped. This activity can be particularly instructive, assisting you in preparing for and growing in similar situations in the future.

Prompt 10. "A conversation I had today that keeps replaying in my mind is..." Examine the specifics of this conversation. What about it that has stayed with you so long? Were there any unspoken emotions or words? Analyzing this can reveal your communication style, desires, and unresolved feelings.

Techniques for Avoiding Judgment and Self-Criticism

Most of us are familiar with that persistent little voice that appears from time to time, often when we least expect or require it. Consider this: You've just completed a project, and while most people would consider it a job well done, all you can think about are the little imperfections. Does this sound familiar? That's your inner critic speaking, and while it may appear to have good intentions at times, its critical nature can hinder our progress.

This voice, where is it coming from? It frequently stems from our earliest formative years. Perhaps it was a parent who had high standards, a teacher who was a stickler for perfection, or peers who were only too happy to call out our mistakes. Our mental conversations are shaped in part by these early encounters. Ironically, we believe that our inner critic is working in our favor. It thinks, in its mistaken way, that it's guiding us toward perfection by highlighting potential hazards. But there's a big difference between helpful criticism and crippling remarks.

Balancing Self-Assessment

The Good

Self-awareness and appraisal are unquestionably beneficial. It enables you to identify areas for growth, set goals, and strive for tremendous success. It's like having a personal coach encouraging you to go the extra mile.

The Bad

When self-evaluation becomes overly negative or derogatory, it is no longer productive. Instead of being a motivator, it becomes a stumbling block that prevents you from reaching your full potential.

Constantly denigrating oneself can lead to low self-esteem and possibly the development of mental health concerns such as anxiety and depression. Constant self-criticism, believe it or not, can appear physically. A lousy self-image can cause stress, sleep difficulties, and reduced immunity.

Instead of attempting new things and taking risks, an overpowering inner critic may force you to play it safe constantly. This results in missed opportunities and impedes personal and professional development.

Taking Steps to Silence the Critic

Recognizing a problem is the first step toward resolving it. Take note of your internal discourse. How frequently is it negative? Are there any triggers? Being aware of these tendencies serves as the foundation for transformation.

When you hear that little voice pointing out flaws, challenge it. "Is this truly constructive?" inquire. Is it true, or is it needless fear?" By challenging the critic, you may lessen its unjustifiable influence.

While it may sound corny, affirmations are effective. Every morning, remind yourself of your talents, accomplishments, and values. These affirmations can assist to drown out the critic over time.

1) Rather than focusing primarily on huge accomplishments, celebrate small successes. Pat yourself on the back for sticking to a new habit for a week or even just getting out of bed on a bad day.

2) Everyone makes mistakes; instead of dwelling on them, forgive, learn from them, and move on.

3) Seek input from trusted friends, family, or colleagues regularly. Most of the time, their assessment of your performance or ability will be far more favorable and balanced than yours.

4) Seek professional help if your inner critic is deeply established, causing major grief. Therapists can provide valuable tools and strategies for reframing negative self-talk.

Remember that changing one's internal discourse is a journey, not a destination. There will be days when the critic is louder than usual, and that's fine. We can all create a healthier, more compassionate connection with ourselves with consistent work, self-awareness, and a dash of self-love. The outside world may be judgmental, but our inner world does not have to be.

Days 11-20: Challenging and Reframing

Cognitive Distortions

Congratulations on surviving the first ten days! The first phase was all about catching those sly negative thoughts, but now it's time to go a little deeper. Over the next ten days, your focus will move to confronting and redefining such beliefs. It's critical to understand cognitive distortions before getting into the procedures; they are our brain's clever ways of convincing us of things that aren't always true. They're like those nefarious gremlins who wreak havoc on our minds. Cognitive distortions are systematic biases in our thinking at its core. Our brain is on autopilot, taking shortcuts when processing information, which might lead to mistakes. Consider driving through a familiar town with an outdated GPS. Sure, you'll get to most places just fine, but the GPS may occasionally take you on a detour, leading you astray. It's similar to your brain experiencing cognitive distortions.

Cognitive distortions are thought patterns that we have often learned over time. They could have evolved due to previous events, upbringing, or even as protection mechanisms. They've served a purpose for many people at some point, perhaps to cope with difficulties. However, if left uncontrolled, they can have an unfavorable impact on our emotions, habits, and decision-making.

Take, for example, an optical illusion museum, where certain rooms make you look like a giant while others shrink you. The rooms warp your perception of reality. Cognitive distortions operate in a similar way, except that your perception of events, yourself, and others is distorted and bent.

To make it a tad clearer, here are some common types:

A. Filtering

Exaggerating the negative features of a situation while ignoring the positive aspects. Many psychologists feel that filtering has its origins in our early experiences. Perhaps a teacher or parent overemphasized our mistakes, making us assume they were more important than our accomplishments. We get stuck in these patterns over time, automatically focusing on the negatives and frequently overlooking the positives.

Filtering can influence:

Relationships: When we constantly focus on our partner's flaws while neglecting their positive characteristics, it's easy to feel discontent.

Work: When we filter out our accomplishments and only notice our faults, we may have emotions of inadequacy or feeling like a failure, even if we are performing well overall.

Mental health: Focusing on the negatives all the time may exacerbate emotions of worry, despair, and low self-esteem.

B. Jumping to Conclusions

One cognitive shortcut our brains enjoy is jumping to conclusions. It's like watching a movie trailer and presuming you know the entire narrative, twists, and finale. While our intuitions can be spot on at times, they can also be far off the mark, resulting in misunderstandings and undue stress.

There are two primary ways in which we jump to conclusions:

Mind Reading: When we believe we know what other people are thinking. For example, if a colleague walks by without greeting you, you might infer they're displeased with you. They could be distracted or are having a bad day.

Fortune Telling: This entails forecasting the future. You might assume, "I'll never get that promotion now," after making a little error in a presentation, even if the reality is far from it.

C. "All-or-Nothing" Thinking

Seeing things in black and white. It's a total failure if something needs improvement. Does this sound familiar? All-or-nothing thinking is motivated by our drive for excellence and our fear of inadequacy. When things don't completely fit with our high standards, it can feel like a huge failure. This way of thinking is prevalent among perfectionists, high performers, and people afraid of being judged.

Consider a student who receives a 90% on a test. Instead of appreciating their accomplishment, they may become fixated on the missed 10%, believing they have failed.

All-or-nothing thinking can have several undesirable consequences:

Stress and Worry: Constantly striving for perfection can be tiring, resulting in burnout and increased anxiety.

Low Self-Esteem: When your efforts are less than ideal, viewing them as complete failures can damage your self-confidence over time.

Inadequate Growth: If you consider every mistake to be a catastrophic failure, you may be less willing to take risks or travel outside of your comfort zone. It can stifle personal and professional development.

Relationship Strains: All-or-nothing thinking can have an impact on interpersonal relationships as well. For example, a minor argument with a loved one may be viewed as the end of a relationship rather than a solvable issue.

D. Catastrophizing: Always Expecting the Worst

Consider this: You're dashing through your daily routine with a cup of coffee when BOOM! The coffee splatters. Instead of dismissing it as a small blunder, a voice in your thoughts says, *"This is a sign. Today is going to be a disaster."* If this seems all too familiar, you've experienced the common cognitive distortion known as "catastrophizing." Catastrophizing, or "magnifying," is assuming the worst-case scenario or constructing a mountain out of a molehill. It's a way of thinking in which little setbacks are interpreted as precursors to more extensive and devastating tragedies. It's not simply a matter of "Oh, I spilled my coffee"; it's also "I spilled my coffee, which means I'm going to be late, which then means I'll miss my first meeting, which will surely get me fired." This distortion snowballs, transforming a single, manageable incident into a series of foreseen disasters.

Why Do We Catastrophize?

Several reasons influence why some of us are more prone to catastrophizing than others.

1)   Past Experiences

If you've been through traumas or severe failures, you may be more sensitive to anticipating them in the future, even if they're unnecessary.

When you experience severe setbacks or traumas in the past, your brain generates an "emotional archive." Consider it a mental filing cabinet where all your experiences are saved and labeled with their associated emotional labels: joyful, sad, traumatic, and so on. When a new event bears even the slightest resemblance to one of those traumatic files, the brain immediately recalls it as a reference point. While this might be useful for avoiding actual threats, it can also lead to catastrophizing when the threat is out of proportion to the reaction.

Because you're more sensitive to anticipating similar setbacks in the future, the anticipation itself might induce tension and anxiety. It has the potential to become a self-fulfilling prophecy. For example, if you are persuaded that you will fail at a task, you may decline to prepare adequately, resulting in the failure you anticipated.

Confirmation Bias

The "Confirmation Bias" is a psychological principle and another factor in catastrophizing. It is our propensity to look for, analyze, and retain data that supports what we currently believe. Thus, if you already believe that "bad things always happen to me," each set of unfortunate events will act as "proof," reinforcing your belief.

The Social and Cultural Perspective

Our cultural background and upbringing, believe it or not, can influence how prior experiences affect us. Some cultures or families place a strong emphasis on caution, risk avoidance, or even pessimism as a type of "preparedness." One may be more prone to catastrophizing if they grew up in such an environment since it has conditioned their brain to anticipate the worst as a means of self-protection.

Coping Mechanisms and Emotional Resilience

How we've been taught to deal with setbacks is also important. You are less prone to catastrophize if you have been trained to view obstacles as learning opportunities. However, if you grew up in an environment where every failure is considered a disaster, your emotional resilience may not have had the chance to develop properly. In this case, previous failures serve as ongoing reminders of "what could go wrong" without the counterbalance of knowing that setbacks can also lead to growth.

Interventions by Professionals and Therapists

Professional assistance, such as therapists or psychologists, can provide a controlled and safe environment to examine and comprehend the underlying causes of these harmful habits. Cognitive Behavioral Therapy {CBT}, for example, guides individuals through techniques that assist them in identifying, understanding, and modifying their distorted thought patterns, teaching them to replace these with more positive and balanced ones. In addition, mindfulness practices emphasize being wholly involved in the here and now, which can shift focus away from anxious foresight and toward a more stable and peaceful mental state. These approaches not only raise awareness of detrimental thought patterns but also provide you with practical tools for confronting and altering them.

2) Anxiety and Depression

One of the common symptoms of these mental health conditions is catastrophizing. It's a vicious circle; nervous thoughts can lead to catastrophizing, which can exacerbate anxiety. Catastrophizing, anxiety, and depression interact in a way that is like a twisted dance trio, with one performer intensifying the movements of the other two. It is intricate and layered, yet no performance anyone wants to participate in. Understanding the players is critical to getting off this mental rollercoaster.

Anxiety: The Perfect Environment for Catastrophizing

First and foremost, let us discuss anxiety. Consider donning spectacles that make you hyper-aware of everything that could go wrong. You're on high alert for pitfalls, spikes, and banana peels with every step you take. That's a good description of how life with anxiety might feel. Anxiety can condition the brain for catastrophizing by keeping it in a state of high alertness, or "hypervigilance." The hypervigilant brain is like a never-sleeping watchdog, constantly evaluating the environment for potential threats. While this response can be helpful in hazardous situations (such as fleeing from a predator), it is less useful in everyday life. The continual state of attention can magnify minor issues into perceived disasters.

The Self-Replicating Cycle of Anxiety

The self-replicating cycle of anxiety is when things become more complicated. Anxiety leads to catastrophizing, which feeds back into anxiety. Consider it a loop or a snowball effect. Assume you're nervous about an upcoming employment interview. This nervousness leads to catastrophizing: "What if I screw up?" What if they despise me? "What if I never get a job?" These terrifying thoughts exacerbate the initial anxiousness, making it even more challenging to prepare for the interview successfully. Of course, if the interview fails to go well, the cycle is repeated: "See?" I knew it was going to be a disaster."

Depression: The Dark Lens of Catastrophizing

Let's now turn the spotlight on the darkest side of human emotion: depression. While anxiety functions as a fuel for catastrophizing, depression operates as fog, darkening the sky even more. Depression is frequently accompanied by a tendency to "globalize" negative experiences, viewing them as proof of universal failure or unworthiness. For example, being passed over for a promotion becomes more than just a professional loss; it becomes proof of total inability. "I'll never be good enough," you believe, setting the stage for even more pessimistic views about your future, relationships, and self-worth. Depression is sometimes accompanied by a sense of hopelessness, as though things would never improve. This fatalistic perspective provides fertile ground for catastrophizing. If you're convinced your future is bleak, it's far easier to picture worst-case scenarios for almost anything. Catastrophizing, like anxiety, can intensify depressed symptoms, plunging you further into a pit of misery.

3) Low Self-Esteem

People with poor self-esteem typically believe they cannot deal with obstacles, leading them to expect the worst when confronted with pressures. They may think they deserve terrible outcomes or are doomed to fail, perpetuating the catastrophizing loop. Let's lift the curtain on this one. Low self-esteem is like carrying around a nagging little critic in your back pocket. This critic questions your every move, convincing you you're unprepared to ride life's roller coaster. Consider this: Every time you face a hurdle, your internal critic grabs the microphone and begins announcing, "Hey, remember that one time you messed up?" You're destined to do it again!"

When you have poor self-esteem, you have a flawed self-perception that selectively focuses on your defects and past failures. You grow more worried because you expect to fail. And when you're nervous, you're more likely to make a mistake. Then, every misstep is interpreted as proof that you are doomed to fail. It's a self-fulfilling prophecy in which your low self-esteem causes you to catastrophize.

4) Social Influences

Your social environment sometimes adds to your predisposition to catastrophize. Growing up in a family whose individuals frequently jump to the worst-case scenario or are surrounded by people who are typically miserable can normalize catastrophizing as a style of thinking. These social cues can have a subtle effect on your psychological patterns.

Everyone is the lead performer in their play, but the scripts occasionally need to be revised. That's right; I'm talking about the people you associate with; family, friends, and even random social media influencers. Have you ever heard the expression, "You are the average of the five people you spend the most time with"? That statement is especially true when it comes to catastrophizing.

Think about this: You're growing up, and the dinner table conversation is no longer about the ordinary "How was your day?" Instead, it's something like, "Did you hear about Cousin Joe?" He lost his job; he's doomed. Doomed, I tell you!" Perhaps your friends always see the bad side of things and make it seem natural to think that way. People around you may encourage your habit of expecting the worst to happen.

Let us consider why this occurs. As social creatures, humans are prone to mimicking; it's how we fit in, learn, and interact with one another. So, if you find yourself in a culture where catastrophizing is the norm, you're likely to adopt the same strategy, perhaps without even recognizing it. This social impact is a concoction of numerous elements, including cultural standards, peer pressure, and, most importantly, the human need for validation. A strange sense of kinship exists when you share a catastrophic thought, and someone else confirms it. Your concern is validated, making it easier to cling to rather than confront. It's a feedback loop; you say something negative, it's repeated, and you're more convinced than ever that you're destined for disaster.

But here's where things get complicated: social media. The infinite scroll might be a breeding ground for your darkest nightmares. Each post and story you read can add to your existing mental framework. A tweet about a layoff here, a blog post about impending doom there, and your already fragile beliefs about your life begin to disintegrate even further.

So, what do you do when you discover your social circle has

become less of a "circle of life" and more of a "vortex of despair"? First and foremost, be aware. Recognizing that your surroundings may contribute to your catastrophizing is half the battle. Be more selective about the voices you allow to affect you. Sometimes, it means having a candid conversation with a constantly negative friend. Other times, it may be necessary to filter your media consumption to include a broader range of opinions. And, sure, that may consist of clicking 'unfollow' on certain doomsayers.

The point is that you have more control over your surroundings than you may believe. If the people around you are as depressing as a bad movie, it's time to adjust. Remember that you control your life and can guide it in any direction.

Combating Catastrophizing

Recognizing your inclination to catastrophize is the first step. Once you're aware of it, you can utilize the following tactics to combat it:

Grounding: Breathing - More Than Just Inhale and Exhale

Let's start with deep breathing, which is the foundation of grounding. "I breathe all the time; what's the big deal?" you may wonder. Intentional deep breathing is more complex than your automatic inhales and exhales. It has been demonstrated that methods such as diaphragmatic breathing or the 4-7-8 method (inhale for 4 seconds, hold for 7, exhale for 8) activate the body's relaxation response, shifting the focus from "fight or flight" to "rest and digest." This physiological change could stop the catastrophizing train in its tracks.

Reality Testing

Consider yourself a checker of your thoughts when engaging in reality testing. You examine what you're thinking carefully to determine if it makes sense. It is not to argue that your feelings are incorrect. Your emotions are always valid. You're challenging the thoughts that make you feel a certain way. You're your detective, gathering evidence to test the accuracy of your catastrophic views.

The Balancing Act

A talent that we commonly apply for multitasking or handling life's obstacles but rarely employ for managing our thought patterns. Our catastrophic thoughts are sometimes only one side of the tale, the worst-case scenario. What about the opposite side? Can we recast the scenario to present it in a more balanced light? We can combat this inclination by practicing mental balance.

First, consider your thought to be a segment of a larger narrative. The plot is created, the action is directed, and the scene is set in your mind. However, it frequently decides to write a tragedy instead of a well-rounded tale with aspects of drama, humor, and sometimes even a happy conclusion. When you become overly anxious, stop and ask yourself, "Is this the entire plot? What other storylines exist?" Just this realization has the potential to alter your ingrained thought habits significantly.

It may seem impossible to reason, much less optimistically, in the heat of the moment. However, as soon as you realize that you're catastrophizing, pause and pose some tough questions to yourself, such as, "What is the real likelihood that the worst-case scenario would occur? Have I already succeeded or handled similar circumstances well? Are there any variables under my control that could alter the result? It's all about expanding your horizons and seeing various options.

Techniques for Questioning the Validity of Negative Thoughts

1) The Socratic Approach: Pose Questions to Yourself

The Socratic Approach is a time-tested method of finding the truth that involves raising and responding to questions and frequently results in a revelation. Consider asking yourself questions such as "What is the evidence for this thought? "Whenever a negative view starts to seep in. Is this a constant? What are the likelihoods that this will occur? Consider how well you've prepared and done in the past and whether you're merely mistaking your uneasiness for lack of preparation.

2) Thought Replacement: Swap it Out

Consider your negative thoughts a lousy song on your mind's radio station. Would you let it play indefinitely or change the channel? Thought replacement is analogous to changing to better music. It entails recognizing and replacing a negative thought with a more productive or realistic one. Replace "I can't do this" with "I will do my best."

3) Testing Your Theory

Regard your negative thinking to be a hypothesis that must be tested. Conduct experiments to confirm or deny it. If you think you're awful at public speaking, put your theory to the test by joining a speaking group or simply making a toast with your friends. You may discover that the evidence needs to support your initial assumption, which will improve your belief system.

4) Observation and Mindfulness

Mindfulness and observation are powerful methods for challenging and breaking negative thoughts' grip on your mind. Being present in the moment is at the heart of mindfulness. It teaches us to live in the present moment without getting caught up in the past or worrying about the future. Previous regrets or future anxieties frequently trigger negative thoughts. We can see these thoughts without being swept away if we anchor ourselves in the present.

Mindfulness encourages nonjudgmental observation of our thoughts and feelings. We begin to understand our thoughts as fleeting occurrences that come and go when we practice detached observation rather than absolute truths. This adjustment in viewpoint helps us to call negative thoughts into question. Rather than taking them at face value, we can ask ourselves, "Is this thought true?" or "Is there another way to look at this situation?"

Many of our negative thought habits are conditioned automatic responses to certain situations. They are frequently reality distortions. They can be overstated, oversimplified, or based on incorrect assumptions. Mindfulness disrupts this automatic cycle by introducing a pause, a moment of awareness in which we can select a different reaction. The belief that everything, including our thoughts and feelings, is transient is a core principle of mindfulness. Recognizing that our unpleasant thoughts are temporary can help reduce their perceived severity and power. Regular mindfulness practice can help you develop control over your emotional responses and cultivate a more transparent, more objective perspective on things. When an unfavorable thought arises, one can immediately return to equilibrium rather than spiraling into greater negativity or fear. Observation enables us to perceive things as they are rather than through the lens of our prejudices or previous experiences.

5) Check in with a Reliable Person

Two heads are sometimes better than one, especially when clouded by negativity. Discuss your opposing viewpoints with a trusted friend, family member, or mentor. They might offer an objective angle that you may have yet to consider.

6) Document and Review

Maintain a thought journal. Make a note of any unpleasant thoughts that come to mind. After a few entries have accumulated, go back, and review them. Is there a repeating theme? Is there any overstated language, such as "always" or "never"? Is the thought the result of a cognitive distortion such as catastrophizing or all-or-nothing thinking?

7) Think about the Long-Term Impact

"Will this matter in a week, a month, or a year?" ask yourself. Zooming out from a broader point of view often sheds new light on the urgency and importance we place on our current negative thoughts.

You're not just mindlessly clicking through your mind's film festival if you use these strategies; you're becoming an engaged, discerning viewer. These abilities allow you to challenge the validity of your views and reinterpret them in a more balanced and helpful manner.

Exercises for Reframing Negative Thoughts into Neutral or Positive Ones

Think of your mind as a canvas covered in abstract strokes of stress, grief, or despair. Wouldn't you want a more balanced image with hints of happiness, joy, or hope? The technique of 'reframing' allows you to repaint that canvas, allowing you to transform your inner environment with a brush and palette. You can convert a messy canvas into a work of art that reflects a more balanced and positive you with deliberate effort and careful color choices. Let's get started!

1) **The Gratitude Strategy: A Remedy for Negative Thought Patterns**

The concept of gratitude has existed for centuries, deeply rooted in diverse cultural and religious traditions. In recent years, there has been a growing focus in scientific research on understanding gratitude's power and its numerous benefits. Research has demonstrated that practicing gratitude can positively impact one's well-being, health, and relationships. Gratitude is a powerful remedy for countering negative thought patterns. When you find yourself caught up in a web of negative thoughts, consider using a structured technique called the Gratitude Strategy. It's not just a diversion strategy; it's a basic mental exercise based on psychological science. The goal is to recall three things you are genuinely grateful for consciously. The guideline in this activity stipulates that you cannot repeat your list; it motivates you to always find fresh parts of your life to admire and be thankful for.

On a neurobiological level, practicing gratitude activates brain regions connected with the neurotransmitter dopamine, also known as the "feel-good" hormone. When you intentionally focus on what you're grateful for, you're reprogramming your brain to detect and emphasize the good, causing a ripple effect that neutralizes or even drowns out negative thoughts. This process of acknowledging and redirecting attention away from negativity can serve as a psychological buffer against stress, anxiety, and depression.

But what does it mean to be grateful? It is more than simply saying "thank you" for something done for you. Gratitude is a complex psychological state characterized by recognizing and appreciating positive and personally significant deeds, events, or even natural features of existence. For some, it may be the love and support of family or friends; for others, it may be the enjoyment of a hobby or the satisfaction of accomplishing a long-desired goal. The definition of appreciation is broad, embracing everything from admiring a magnificent sunset to recognizing a longstanding partnership.

It's critical to understand that thankfulness is a process and a regular way of viewing the world rather than a feeling. Consider it a lens that lets you see things in your life more fully. The glass gets more apparent as you practice thankfulness, allowing you to see the benefits that your negative thoughts would have obscured.

When you have a terrible thought and feel its negative energy dragging you down, stop and consciously think of three things you're thankful for. Write them down; writing has been demonstrated to strengthen cognitive processes. This simple but effective exercise will develop a mental balance to your negative thought habits. It resets your emotional state, lessening the urgency and depth of your initial negativity.

Incorporating the Gratitude Strategy into daily routines can yield long-term advantages. By practicing thankfulness regularly, you can cultivate a "gratitude attitude," which makes you more inclined to recognize and value the good things in your life. Gratitude can develop into an endless cycle over time: the more you find reasons to be thankful, the more opportunities you find to express gratitude. Thus, the Gratitude Strategy is powerful and well-recognized for counteracting negative thought patterns.

Gratitude's neurobiological and psychological benefits minimize the impacts of negativity and enrich your mental and emotional health. By implementing this simple yet profoundly transformational practice into your life, you lay the framework for being the type of person who can find joy, happiness, and meaning even amid adversity and disappointments.

2) The "If, then" Technique: Creating New Routes Through Your Mind's Maze

Getting caught up in a cycle of unfavorable thoughts that foretell unpleasant events is typical. These aren't just negative thoughts; they can impact our actions and hinder our ability to enjoy life or make sensible decisions. The "If, then" technique, based on Cognitive Behavioral Therapy (CBT), is one successful way to break out of this loop. CBT teaches that our thoughts, feelings, and actions are interrelated and that changing one can influence others.

Let's use this strategy on something familiar: a first date. Assume you're getting ready to go out with someone you're interested in, and you have the following thought: "If I show my true self, I won't be liked." This thinking can function like a dark cloud, casting a shadow over your natural charisma and making you mistrust every word or movement you say or do. The key issue here isn't just the initial negative thought; it can trigger a chain reaction.

Suppose you're worried that being yourself will make you unlikable. In that case, the anxiety can impact your behavior, causing you to appear guarded or inauthentic, which may cause the date to be less successful.

The "If, then" technique encourages questioning of your automatic thoughts. Rather than accepting your first negative idea as your fate, ask yourself, "Is this the only possible outcome?" It's only sometimes the case. So, the most crucial component of this strategy is coming up with alternate endings for your "If, then" statements. Instead of continuing to say, "If I show my true self, I won't be liked," why not think, "If I show my true self, they might appreciate my uniqueness," or "If I show my true self, I'll attract someone who likes me for who I am"? This exercise isn't meant to convince you that these alternate scenarios will occur but rather to remind you that they could—the narrative shifts from impending doom to possibility.

The benefits of creating these alternate scenarios are numerous:

✓ **It breaks your negative thought monopoly, allowing for a more neutral or optimistic approach.**

✓ **It provides a more balanced view of the problem, improving decision-making.**

✓ **It validates your ability to control your reactions and emotions.**

How will you put this into action? It all starts with becoming conscious of your thought patterns. Give yourself a mental pause the next time a negative "If, then" statement enters your mind. Please take a deep breath to establish a space between your idea and initial reaction. Examine the original thought's validity in this space. Make a list of possible outcomes; feel free to write them down if it helps you think about them more deeply.

Though it may appear simple, it is sometimes difficult to practice at first. Even when the thought patterns are harmful, our minds tend to stick to them. However, like any skill, practice makes perfect. The more you use it, the more natural it will become to consider other outcomes when confronted with a negative "If, then" statement.

The "If, then" technique focuses on mental progress rather than thought replacement. You're not deleting the negative and penciling it in a positive; you're broadening and balancing your internal story. This training promotes a more adaptable, flexible mindset, a vital advantage in the intricate network of thoughts, emotions, and experiences that characterize our existence.

3) **Reversing Thought Patterns Using the 'Flip It' Exercise**

If you've ever been caught up in a negative thought cycle, you know how they may exaggerate a problem, making it appear worse than it is. A "Flip It" exercise is a helpful method for changing this dynamic. This strategy originated in cognitive psychology and serves as a vital tool for intercepting automatic negative thoughts, giving a refreshing new perspective. It's incredible how merely changing our thinking may cause a difference in our emotional state.

The core concept is straightforward: invert a negative belief. Instead of embracing the idea as absolute fact, challenge it and flip it to represent a positive or neutral viewpoint. For example, if you think, "I'll never get this job," ask yourself, "Why shouldn't I get this job?" The next essential step after flipping the thought is to challenge oneself to create arguments for this new, flipped thought. It isn't just a routine activity; it's a cognitive reorganization exercise. Allow yourself the time and mental space to consider why the flipped view is valid. You may have the necessary skill set for the position, previously held similar roles, or your educational background matches the work criteria. You may have spent significant time preparing for the interview, researching the firm, practicing your responses, and even practicing your body language.

Alternatively, you may bring a unique viewpoint to the position that will make you an addition to the team: you might highlight specific experiences, projects, or attributes that set you apart from other candidates.

This activity fulfills multiple purposes. For starters, it breaks the loop of negativity. Once you've successfully "flipped" an idea, the original negative belief frequently loses much of its emotional intensity, making it more straightforward to address the matter more objectively. Second, finding arguments for the flipped thought aids in balancing your viewpoint. You are not disregarding potential obstacles; instead, you realize these are not the only possible outcomes. Finally, this activity might increase your self-esteem and self-efficacy by reminding you of your abilities, achievements, or worth.

Like any ability, the "Flip It" method improves with constant practice. Flipping a firmly ingrained negative thought may initially feel awkward or unnatural. However, the more you practice it, the more natural it will become, and you may notice that positive or neutral ideas begin to appear more spontaneously.

The "Flip It" exercise isn't limited to job-related concerns; it's a versatile tool that can be used in a variety of situations, including social interactions ("Why would anyone want to talk to me?" to "Why wouldn't people want to talk to me?"), health-related concerns, and even general worries about your future.

It is a systematic approach to testing and modifying your habitual thought habits. Using this strategy regularly can build a more balanced view of the problems and opportunities ahead, allowing you to approach them with greater confidence and less worry.

4) Metaphor Makeover: Reframing Life Using Different Analogies

The metaphors we use to explain our lives can significantly impact our emotional state, how we approach situations, and even our fundamental belief systems. The words and images we choose to express complicated experiences do more than explain them; they actively influence them. This phenomenon is so important that it has been investigated in various fields, including psychology, linguistics, and philosophy.

Consider the metaphor of life as a "battle." This story may evoke feelings of perpetual struggle, conflict, and opposition. When you approach each day as if it were a fresh combat in a continuing war, the underlying tension and anger can infiltrate every connection. Challenges may be interpreted as threats, mistakes as failures, and others as allies or rivals. The "us vs. them" mentality accompanying this metaphor may create a chronic sense of antagonism, draining the joy and fulfillment of everyday encounters. While this 'war' metaphor may be energizing and uplifting for some, it can be tiring and restrictive for others.

Now, consider changing the metaphor to describe life as a "journey." Suddenly, difficulties become markers to be navigated, experiences become lessons, and others become fellow travelers or guides. The "journey" metaphor has an intrinsic fluidity and movement that allows growth, change, and surprise. Mistakes are no longer debilitating setbacks but rather detours or opportunities for learning. The perspective of life as a journey might facilitate an easier acceptance of imperfection and uncertainty, which many people find mentally and emotionally liberating.

Alternatively, consider life a "dance," which encompasses the concepts of rhythm, grace, and collaboration. When life is viewed as a dance, the emphasis moves to timing, flow, and harmony. Challenges evolve into a complex series of motions requiring skill to perform. There's also a collaborative element here: you're part of a broader, flowing spectacle in which the other participants are neither your opponents nor your allies but your co-dancers. The emphasis is on maintaining balance, composure, and coordination rather than overcoming difficulties.

How does one go about putting this "Metaphor Makeover" into action? First, discover the dominant metaphor you've been applying to your life unconsciously (or consciously). Are you in a fight, a race, a maze, or another situation? Next, consider how well this metaphor serves you. Does it strengthen you, or does it cause you unnecessary tension, anxiety, or negativity? After you've examined your default metaphor, explore alternatives that may better reflect your beliefs, objectives, and the emotional tone you want to set for your life.

Finally, try to actively apply your new metaphor to different elements of your life. For example, if you use the "journey" metaphor and run into an issue at work, visualize it as a steep hill you must climb. Determine what you'll need to go to the top, whether extra talents, aid from others, or more time. The more you apply your chosen metaphor to various life circumstances, the more established this new way of thinking will become. This method has the potential to profoundly affect your emotional experiences, decision-making processes, and interactions with people over time.

5)   **The Benefits and Drawbacks of the Objective Eye Method**

When you're hooked on an unpleasant thought that won't go away, it can help you to take a step back and assess it honestly. The "Pros and Cons: The Objective Eye" method, which entails constructing a basic two-column list, is one successful way to accomplish this. List the 'Pros' or benefits of holding on to this negative mindset on one side. List the 'Cons' or downsides on the other side.

Here's how to do it:

Take a piece of paper or use a digital note app to envision your thoughts better, write them down, or type them out. It allows you to withdraw from the emotional pull of negative thinking and see things more clearly and balanced.

Create two columns: one labeled 'Pros' and the other 'Cons'.

List the Benefits: List any advantages or benefits of sustaining your negative belief in the 'Pros' section. For example, if your thought is, "I'll never get promoted," a 'pro' could be that believing this prevents you from feeling disappointed later.

Disadvantages: List all the disadvantages of holding on to this concept in the 'Cons' section. Continuing with the previous example, a 'con' could be that this thought prevents you from providing your best effort at work or dampens your enthusiasm to develop new abilities, lowering your prospects of advancement.

Evaluate: Once your list is finished, look at both columns. Often, the disadvantages of holding on to negative thoughts exceed the benefits. You may find it challenging to consider any 'benefits.' This exercise assists you in identifying the absurdity or imbalance in your first belief and provides a fact-based reason to let it go.

Reflect: Give some thought to the 'Cons' you've stated. These are the exact ways this belief harms or impedes you. You may discover that simply writing things down reduces the power of the concept over you.

Act: If the cons outnumber the pros, take this as a wake-up call to confront this negative thought more firmly in your daily life. Consider how you can oppose it by making positive affirmations or obtaining evidence that contradicts the thought.

This method's main advantages are its simplicity and objectivity. It cuts through the emotional cloud surrounding a tenacious concept and helps you weigh the Pros and Cons. The Objective Eye Method adds logic to the issue and puts you back in charge, giving you the necessary perspective to reassess and frequently discard troublesome thinking.

6)   **The Reality Anchor: An Evidence-Based Approach to Overcoming Negative Thoughts**

Negative thoughts have a habit of taking on a life of their own, spiraling out of control and throwing a cloud over our emotional well-being. It's easy to lose sight of the bigger, more balanced picture of our life in such times. The "Reality Anchor" method is intended to help you root yourself, counteracting the emotional tornado created by negativity.

What Exactly Is a Reality Anchor?

The Reality Anchor is an absolute, positive truth or event you may focus on. This anchor can be anything in your life that is unequivocally true and positive.

Here are several examples:

Past Achievements: Recall a time when you excelled at anything, whether it was finishing a job at work, reaching a fitness goal, or gaining acknowledgment for an accomplishment.

Stable Relationships: Identify a relationship in your life that provides you with comfort and support, whether it is with a family member, a friend, or a loving partner.

Kindness: Think about a recent act of kindness you performed or received. Small gestures can often have a significant emotional impact.

Skills or Talents: Consider a skill or talent that makes you feel competent and valuable.

How to Use the Reality Anchor

Identify the Anchor: First, determine your reality anchor, which is a positive, unarguable fact that you cannot refute. Remember this data or write it down on paper or a digital note for easy reference.

Pause: When you find yourself drawn into a vortex of negative thoughts, deliberately decide to pause. Take a deep breath to disengage from your habitual thoughts and emotional responses.

Focus: Bring your Reality Anchor into focus. Recall the event, relationship, or activity that you've chosen vividly. Consider the specifics, conversations, sensations, or any other validation that anchors this reality.

Counterbalance: Use your Reality Anchor to confront the current unpleasant thought or feeling you're having. Consider how this uplifting truth interacts with your unfavorable ideas. Does it provide a fresh viewpoint or challenge the broad generalizations that negative thoughts frequently bring with them?

Reinforce: Use this opportunity to emphasize that your life is not a one-dimensional canvas painted in hues of negativity. This positive fact shows that your predicament is not as severe as your initial impressions suggest, implying that your situation may be less painful than anticipated.

Continue the Dialogue: Remind yourself of your Reality Anchor whenever negative ideas arise. This regular reinforcement will help you to stay grounded through emotional storms.

Document the Process: Some people find it helpful to keep a notebook or log in which they record instances of successfully employing their Reality Anchor. You'll amass a library of positive information and experiences you can refer to over time, making the method more successful.

The Reality Anchor approach works because it takes advantage of a psychological concept known as cognitive dissonance. This term alludes to the mental tension or unease when we simultaneously have two opposing concepts. When you bring solid, positive information into focus alongside an unfavorable concept, your mind experiences tension and is compelled to examine the accuracy of the negative thought.

Simply put, the appearance of a positive fact calls into question the all-negative story you may be feeding yourself. This mental conflict forces your mind to reconcile the two competing points of view. As a result, the technique pushes you to think in a more multidimensional manner, assisting you in moving away from immediate emotional suffering and toward a balanced and sensible frame of mind.

7) **Emotional Alchemy: Turning Negative Feelings into Positive Strengths**

"Emotional Alchemy" is the purposeful reframing of the emotions that fuel your thoughts. The idea is to determine which emotion is driving a given thought. This emotion can range from fear of failure to jealousy over someone else's accomplishments, or it might be melancholy associated with a sense of loss. Then, consider how to turn that emotion into a strength.

Let's break down this concept. The first and most crucial step is correctly describing this emotion since doing so gives you a well-defined starting point for transformation. Identifying the feeling allows you to separate it, making it easier to confront rather than allowing it to swirl in the background of your thoughts. What's important to realize is that you're not attempting to dismiss or minimize the emotion you're experiencing. You're not suggesting it's "wrong" or "bad" to have these feelings. Instead, you're looking at the same emotion from a new perspective to determine whether it might be beneficial in specific scenarios. By doing so, you reduce the negative impact the emotion has on your thoughts by also considering the positive that it can bring.

Once you've identified the underlying emotion, consider how that emotion could be beneficial. It's equivalent to transforming something negative into something positive. For example, if you're worried or fearful, consider how being scared might make you more cautious and help you plan better. Instead of viewing emotion as a negative, think about how it may help you be more careful, double-check your work, or prepare better.

Let's take the emotion "fear" as an example to explain this further. Assume you have an important project deadline and are terrified of not finishing it on time. This dread may cause you to feel uncomfortable, pressured, and unsure of your abilities. You may begin to postpone because your fear has convinced you that you will fail anyway. Fear has a negative impact on your thoughts as well as your behavior in this situation.

Instead of dismissing or undermining this concern (after all, tasks are essential, and deadlines are real), you try to look at it from a different perspective. "In what situation could this fear be helpful?" you wonder.

You may discover that anxiety makes you more attentive to details, forcing you to double-check your work. It may make you more disciplined in sticking to a timetable to meet the deadline. This anxiety may inspire you to go above and beyond to make a decent endeavor into a fantastic one.

By examining these positive qualities, you are not denying that fear may be paralyzing; instead, you understand that fear, in the appropriate context, can be stimulating and inspiring. You're pushing the boundaries of what the emotion "fear" means to you, evaluating both its constructive and destructive potential.

So, instead of being entirely paralyzed by your anxiety, you may now reduce its adverse effect on your thinking. You can think more clearly and operate more effectively, not because the fear has disappeared but because you better understand it. You're harnessing the same emotion that could paralyze you to encourage you to finish your project successfully.

The Role of Affirmations and Visualization

Your mind is an intriguing and intricate network of thoughts, ideas, and emotions. It might be your most valuable ally, generating creative concepts and solutions. It may, however, be your harshest critic, trapping you in a cycle of negative thinking that undermines your well-being and productivity. What resources can you draw on to break free and redirect your thoughts to a more constructive path when caught in this mental cloud of negativity? Affirmations and visualizations are two powerful approaches to consider. They act as guideposts, assisting you in navigating the intricate details of your thoughts, particularly when you wander into negative or self-defeating territory.

Affirmations are positive words that have the potential to empower, transform, and heal. They are short, potent statements that direct your conscious and subconscious thoughts toward a desired outcome. Affirmations are much more than catchy phrases or feel-good slogans to repeat in front of a mirror; they are strategic psychological tools that can create your reality.

Based on various scientific disciplines, such as psychology, cognitive neuroscience, and behavioral science, affirmations are empowering words that can assist you in confronting and overcoming negative and self-defeating ideas.

They are designed to impact both your conscious and subconscious mind, leading them toward a desired outcome or state of being. Usually expressed in the first person and in the present tense, such as "I am confident," "I am strong," or "I attract positive energy." These comments are intended to challenge and replace negative self-talk and act as a vocal expression of the qualities, circumstances, or achievements you aspire to.

Let us first analyze the process by which affirmations exert their influence. Cognitive psychologists believe that our thoughts influence our emotions and actions. When you are locked in a loop of negative thinking, it frequently leads to a self-fulfilling prophecy in which your negative expectations influence your activities so that those predictions come true. For example, if you continuously tell yourself that you're "not good at public speaking," you're more likely to become apprehensive before a presentation, which will destroy your performance, confirming your original opinion. Affirmations seek to disrupt this cycle by substituting negative thought patterns with positive ones.

To understand how affirmations work deeper, consider the two systems of conscious and subconscious thought. Your conscious mind is logical and analytical, capable of reasoning through complex problems. Your subconscious mind, on the other hand, relies on intuition and deeply ingrained beliefs. These beliefs are generally formed over years, if not decades, due to experiences, education, and the people around you. The strength of affirmations resides in their ability to gradually permeate your subconscious mind, changing old beliefs and making space for positive thoughts, feelings, and behaviors.

Affirmations are dynamic when combined with other cognitive behavioral strategies like visualization. As you repeat your selected affirmation, "I am worthy," imagine yourself feeling and acting as though you are truly worthy. Imagine effectively resolving a challenging situation, whether at work or in a personal relationship. Consider yourself acting confidently, making solid decisions, and being regarded with respect by others. This vivid mental rehearsal amplifies the power of the affirmation, increasing the likelihood that you'll embody that sense of worthiness in real-life settings.

Creating the Best Affirmations

Affirmations must be personal, precise, and believable to be effective. Replace a negative mindset like, "I'm terrible at public speaking," with an affirmation like, "I am growing more confident in public speaking every day." This statement is not only positive; it is also actionable and forward-thinking. Particular affirmations that relate to your life experiences are the most effective. Affirmations such as "I am happy" may be beneficial, but personalizing an affirmation to address specific difficulties or goals will usually create more apparent effects. For example, if you want to improve your assertiveness, an affirmation like "I speak my mind with clarity and confidence" would be more appropriate than just saying "I am confident."

Daily positive affirmations can result in profound transformation, illuminating the route to desired change in numerous areas of your life, including emotional, mental, physical, and even spiritual. Multiple research studies have found that this exercise helps reduce stress, promote general happiness, boost self-esteem, and improve problem-solving abilities in those who are stressed.

However, affirmations are most potent when used correctly, like any tool. Incorporating affirmations into your daily routine is one of the most effective methods to harness the power of affirmations. The foundation of habit-building is consistency. You can't expect to become physically fit by going to the gym once a month or changing your thought patterns without constant and frequent practice. By using affirmations daily, you reinforce a new, positive belief system and develop a daily habit of positive thinking.

How could you incorporate affirmations into your routine? Here are a few approaches to consider:

Morning and Evening Rituals

Begin and conclude your day by saying aloud your chosen affirmations. Imagine waking up and thinking, "Today will be a great day." Starting your day with a positive affirmation can help set the tone for the rest of your day. Take a few moments after you wake up to speak your chosen affirmations out loud. Affirmations can be done while stretching, preparing your morning coffee, or showering. It creates a chain reaction of happy thoughts and behaviors throughout the day. Attaching your affirmations to everyday activities is the most superb method to ensure you remember to recite them. For example, you can recite an affirmation whenever you brush your teeth. This strategy, also known as habit stacking, guarantees you remember to utilize your affirmations.

Post-it notes with affirmations on your bathroom mirror, computer display, or refrigerator might be a helpful reminder. You may also set automated reminders on your phone or computer to remind you to say an affirmation at specified moments.

Repeat your affirmations as you prepare to sleep. This technique can help cleanse the mind of negativity gathered throughout the day, ensuring that you sleep with a happy and calm perspective.

Why Do We Say Affirmations Aloud?

When you vocalize something, you are reinforcing it through several channels. Not only are you thinking about the idea, but you're also hearing it and experiencing the physical act of creating the words. This multi-sensory experience helps in the integration of the affirmation into your consciousness. Saying affirmations aloud necessitates active engagement, which increases your involvement in the process. This active involvement keeps your attention from wandering and keeps you focused on the affirmation. There is a distinction between hearing a sentence in your mind and hearing it with your ears. Affirmations become more "real" to the brain when they are spoken. When you say the words aloud, they have additional weight and conviction. On a more profound spiritual or metaphysical level, it is claimed that saying positive affirmations boosts one's vibratory frequency, bringing you closer to your goals and ambitions.

Incorporating affirmations into your daily routine is a systematic way to reshape your mind, dispelling negative thoughts and reinforcing positivity. While thinking affirmations are helpful, repeating them aloud activates various neural pathways, assuring a deeper and more lasting impact. As with any self-improvement strategy, the key is consistency, dedication, and faith in the process.

Written Exercise:

Writing your affirmations down might help to cement them in your memory, making them more likely to be followed. The process of committing thoughts to paper (or screen) has been acknowledged for its several advantages. Writing can dramatically increase the efficacy of affirmations. Let's look at why writing can be especially beneficial. Writing stimulates the brain in a different way than simply thinking or speaking. We create a visual representation of our thoughts when we write things down. This visual cue improves memory recall. As you repeatedly write down the same affirmation, it becomes embedded in your memory, making it more straightforward to recall and reflect on even when you are not actively engaged with the written affirmation.

Writing is a physical act. A sense of commitment is made as your hand goes across the paper or as you type out the words. By writing your affirmations, you are essentially establishing a covenant with yourself. Each pen stroke or key press is an affirmation in and of itself, a meaningful step toward beneficial transformation. Writing requires concentration. This focused effort ensures that your full attention is on the affirmation. You analyze each word, internalizing its meaning more thoroughly than if you were reciting it. This in-depth reflection ensures that the affirmation is more than a surface phrase but something you truly understand and relate to.

A written affirmation is a permanent record. As you reread your written affirmations, you can see your progress, reflect on how your sentiments or beliefs have grown, and use past affirmations as encouragement or inspiration. This permanent record serves as evidence of your journey, the actions you've taken, and the beliefs you've developed.

Your subconscious mind is crucial in creating your thoughts and behaviors. It is continually absorbing information and making connections. Writing affirmations down sends a clear message to your mind. As this message is repeated consistently, your subconscious accepts it as accurate, progressively affecting deep-seated beliefs and thought patterns.

Writing is therapeutic for many people. When you write down your affirmations, you're logging positive statements and releasing any related feelings. If your affirmation is, "I am deserving of love and respect," writing it down may trigger feelings of past harm, reaffirmation of self-worth, or hope for the future. The affirmation becomes even more powerful by connecting with these feelings since it is grounded in actual emotion.

It helps to visualize what you've written when you read it back.

For example, if your affirmation is about accomplishing a specific goal, having it in writing might help you understand the processes required, potential hurdles, and ultimate success. Visualization, in turn, increases motivation and commitment to your affirmation.

Writing down affirmations is a dynamic activity that involves the brain, the subconscious, and emotions. By putting affirmations to paper, you are consolidating them in your mind, making them an essential part of your thought process, and raising the possibility that they will affect your actions and behaviors in a good way.

Trigger Points

Affirmation "trigger points" function similarly to reminders. Some occasions or events prompt you to say or think about your positive affirmation. It's comparable to how we may salivate when seeing our favorite cuisine since we've learned to identify that dish with a good experience. By employing these reminders (trigger points) to say our affirmations regularly, we will quickly find that the reminder alone can cause us to think or act more positively.

Let's take this one step at a time:

Step 1. Choosing Trigger Points

The initial step is identifying appropriate trigger points related to the affirmation you're working with. For example, if your affirmation is related to confidence, such as "I am capable and ready for any challenge," appropriate trigger points could include entering a conference room or starting a challenging task.

Step 2. Consistent Pairing

Once you've discovered your trigger points, the next step is to say or reflect on your affirmation whenever you encounter one. For example, you could pause momentarily before entering a conference room, take a deep breath, and mentally repeat your affirmation.

Step 3. The Power of Repetition

The more you identify a specific trigger with your affirmation, the more firmly ingrained that affirmation becomes in your consciousness. This repetition strengthens positive thought and enhances the possibility of the affirmation impacting your behavior and emotional response in the appropriate situation.

Step 4. Expanding Trigger Points

As you become more acclimated to employing trigger points, you may notice other events or occasions that can act as new triggers. It allows you to apply the benefits of affirmations to different elements of your life, ensuring a more holistic approach to positive self-talk.

Step 5. Tangible Reminders

You can utilize tangible reminders to improve the impact of trigger points. Affirmation Cards, for example. These are little cards, like business cards, with your affirmation printed or scribbled on them. Carry one in your pocket or purse, stick one on your car's dashboard, or tuck one inside the cover of a notepad or planner you use frequently. When you come across these cards throughout the day, take a minute to halt, read the affirmation out loud (or in your head if the situation does not allow for speaking), and absorb its message. A relationship card can say, "Today, I choose understanding and patience with my partner."

Trigger points serve as anchors for positive self-talk throughout the day. They provide an organized method of introducing affirmations into your life through regular practice so that you may make positive self-talk a habit and a significant component of how you react to situations or obstacles.

Examples of Trigger Points in Daily Life

Morning Routine

After brushing your teeth in the morning, recite your affirmation briefly. It sets a pleasant tone for the rest of the day. Affirmation example: "Today, I embrace love, understanding, and patience in all my interactions."

Phone Unlocking

Take a deep breath and softly recite your affirmation each time you open your phone before drilling into your apps. It can be a constant reminder throughout the day. Affirmation example: "I value and cherish the connections I have in my life."

Entering Your Home

As a trigger point, use the action of unlocking and opening your front door or garage door. Before entering, consider the environment you want to establish or maintain in your home. Affirmation example: "I bring positivity, peace, and love into my home."

Before Going to Bed

Reflect on the day and recite your affirmation while you switch off the bedside lamp or charge your phone. Reflection aids in closing the day on a pleasant note. Affirmation example: "I am grateful for the love and support I share and receive."

Trigger Points and Affirmations for Relationships ~ Partnerships:

Waking up next to your partner

Affirmation: "I am grateful for another day with you."

Before a difficult conversation

Affirmation: "I will approach this conversation with empathy and understanding."

When you are feeling misunderstood

Affirmation: "I will communicate my feelings clearly and listen to my partner's perspective."

After a long day, before going to bed

Affirmation: "Our bond strengthens with each challenge we overcome."

When there is a disagreement

Affirmation: "I choose love over being right."

When spending meaningful time with one another

Affirmation: "These moments reinforce our bond and connection."

When separated for an extended period

Affirmation: "Distance only strengthens our bond."

When recalling old memories or viewing old photographs

Affirmation: "We have built a wealth of shared experiences together."

When you are feeling insecure in your relationship

Affirmation: "Our love is steadfast and secure."

Before making a mutual decision

Affirmation: "We make the best decisions when we collaborate and trust one another."

When celebrating an anniversary or important date

Affirmation: "Every day with you is a testament to our enduring love."

Before attending social gatherings or meeting up with friends

Affirmation: "Together, we bring out the best in each other."

When planning for the future

Affirmation: "Our future is bright because we created it together."

During physical affectionate moments (e.g., hugging, holding hands)

Affirmation: "Our love is real and present in every touch."

When confronted with external obstacles or stressors

Affirmation: "Together, we can weather any storm."

Tips:

Personalize Your Affirmations: The affirmations listed above are broad. They must resonate with your unique experiences and sentiments to be effective. Customize them to represent the specific circumstances of your relationship.

Repeat Frequently: The more you repeat your affirmations, particularly during the relevant trigger periods, the more they influence your relationship, mindset, and conduct.

Believe in Them: Affirmations are only effective if you believe in your words. Even if it feels uncomfortable initially, these optimistic affirmations can transform your mentality with time and repetition.

You may develop positive thinking, better communication, and a closer link with your partner by associating affirmations with certain moments or trigger points in your relationship.

Visualization: Using Imagination to Spark Creativity

If affirmations are your internal dialogue's vocabulary, visualization is the theater where your mind practices real-life scenarios. This technique requires you to construct mental images, situations, or movies that reflect desired outcomes. Athletes frequently utilize this strategy to "see" themselves winning races or scoring goals before the event.

Affirmations and visualizations combine to give your goals more depth, texture, and emotional color. An affirmation might include "I am calm and centered." A similar image or visualization that may complement this affirmation may involve imagining yourself in a peaceful place where you can feel the sun on your face, hear the sound of a stream, and feel your heartbeat slow down.

Understanding Visualization

The act of constructing a detailed mental image of a desired outcome or scenario is known as visualization. It's like imagining yourself as both a film's director and the star. But it's not just any film; it induces genuine emotional responses from you since your brain interprets these imagined circumstances in the same way that it does actual experiences.

The brain is a complicated and complex organ, yet despite its sophistication, it can't always differentiate what's real and vividly imagined. When you close your eyes and visualize, the same areas of your brain light up as if you were experiencing the event.

Neuroimaging technologies, such as fMRI and EEG, have been used in studies to discover that the brain patterns active during visualization closely reflect the patterns activated during actual performance or experience. These technologies show that the brain does not distinguish between a powerfully imagined and an authentic experience. Because of this phenomenon, athletes, performers, and successful people from many walks of life employ visualization techniques to improve their skills, raise their confidence, and prepare for events.

Our minds are flexible. Regular and repetitive imagery can develop neuronal connections in the brain, "wiring" it to be more inclined toward the results we envision. With persistent imagery, the brain can be trained to accomplish specific activities or naturally adopt certain behaviors over time.

To comprehend the power of visualization, imagine the universe as a vast sea of vibrations. At its heart, everything, from the chair you're sitting on to the emotions you feel, is energy vibrating at different frequencies. When you are thinking or feeling something, you emit a vibratory frequency. Visualization, then, is more than merely conjuring up mental images. It's all about tuning into the frequency of your intended world. You're not just seeing something when you vividly picture it; you're feeling it, immersing yourself in its energy, and aligning your frequency with it.

The visualization process links the non-physical realm of thought and our physical world. By retaining an idea in your mind and infusing it with emotion regularly, you signal your objectives clearly to the universe. The more vivid and emotionally intense your visualization, the stronger its magnetic pull in attracting comparable energies or manifestations to you. Consider this: every time you visualize, you are planting seeds in the fertile land of the universe. The emotions you experience serve as the water that nourishes these seedlings. With persistent attention and intention, these seeds can sprout and grow over time, materializing in your physical reality.

It is not only a matter of manifesting material aspirations. Visualization can be a powerful tool for personal development and healing. Visualizing scenarios where you act with confidence, generosity, or any other desirable characteristic trains new behavioral patterns in your mind's safe area. These habits can gradually replace old, limiting ideas and actions, resulting in actual personal development.

Visualization's Quantum Mechanics: Bridging Thoughts and Reality

Visualization is a powerful cognitive tool, but its origins may be more connected with reality than previously imagined. Enter the fascinating world of quantum physics, a research branch investigating the universe's smallest particles. This branch of physics may appear distant from the art of visualization, but it converges in intriguing ways.

Everything in the universe is energy on the tiniest scale. Because our thoughts result from brain networks and electrical impulses, they are also forms of energy. Particles in quantum physics can become "entangled" (referred to as "quantum entanglement"), which means that the state of one particle is reliant on the form of another, regardless of distance.

Consider your thoughts to be energy forms. When you engage in deep visualization, you are not merely producing random, temporary images. You're thinking in a focused, energetic manner. We believe these patterns can affect or become "entangled" with the universe's energy through a process we don't fully comprehend.

There is a scientific concept known as "quantum field theory." Everything is said to be formed of microscopic fields, like a vast, invisible blanket. And all the specks of dust we see are just little jumps or wiggles in this blanket. Our thoughts now have energy. If these thoughts come into contact with the blanket, they may cause it to wriggle differently. As a result, it's reasonable to believe that they could alter the field's excitations, consequently influencing reality.

You create repeated energy patterns by envisioning a specific outcome, concept, or emotion. Suppose these patterns are stable and consistent enough over time. In that case, quantum mechanics says they could influence the quantum fields surrounding us, increasing the likelihood of the anticipated outcome in our lived experience.

How Does Visualization Affect Reality?

By mentally rehearsing potential outcomes or scenarios, you are not merely daydreaming. You're conditioning your brain to get acquainted with these scenarios. Over time, your brain begins to believe that what you're picturing can (or has already) become a reality.

For example, if you envision yourself confidently presenting a presentation at work, your brain tends to correlate that scenario with emotions of confidence and accomplishment. The more you imagine it, the more "real" it becomes to your mind. As a result, when the big day approaches, you'll be more confident because you've done it successfully multiple times.

Meditation and Visualization

When visualization is paired with meditation, it becomes much more powerful. But how are the two linked? Meditation is a practice in which you focus your mind, usually through guided imagery or concentrating on your breath, to create a state of deep relaxation and heightened awareness. When you meditate, you are reducing the buzz and commotion of everyday thoughts, which are typically clouded by worry, anxiety, or negativity.

In this relaxed condition, your body releases stress and tension, giving it an excellent atmosphere for visualization. Your visualization skills improve because there are fewer distractions when your mind is quiet. Images become more apparent, sharper, and more vivid. They don't have to fight through layers of daily concerns or stray thoughts.

Consider this in the context of removing negative thoughts. When you're comfortable, the barricades we typically erect out of skepticism, self-doubt, or prior disappointments soften or disappear. This openness allows positive visions to take root deep within our subconscious, strengthening positive thoughts and challenging negative ones.

Negative thought patterns frequently feel like an endless cycle in our heads, encouraging self-doubt and limiting beliefs. This process can be broken through visualization.

By imagining optimistic scenarios or saying positive affirmations regularly, you're reprogramming your brain to favor optimism. This exercise can lower the frequency and intensity of negative thoughts over time. You begin to write a new story for yourself, one filled with optimism, hope, and self-belief.

Detoxifying your mind using affirmations and visualizations entails replacing negative, toxic thoughts with positive, uplifting ones. When you purge negativity from your mind, you're effectively draining out mental "toxins" and replenishing your cognitive reservoir with clean, pure concepts.

Mental cleansing is a continuous process. Create a daily routine in which you practice affirmations and visualizations for a few minutes in the morning and at the end of the day.

Keep a journal where you can write down any reoccurring negative thoughts and how you've dealt with them using affirmations and visualizations. You'll see patterns over time and be able to adjust your methods accordingly.

Affirmations and visualizations are practical tools for breaking the cycle of negative thinking. By intentionally and actively challenging and changing your beliefs, you eliminate the clutter and lay the groundwork for optimism to grow. Both strategies rely on your mind's ability to change and adapt, providing a practical, scientifically supported method of achieving emotional well-being. If you make these techniques a regular part of your mental hygiene, you'll notice that the clouds of negativity begin to split, allowing the sunshine of positivity to show through.

Days 21-30: Developing Positivity

Following the initial stages of self-awareness and introspection, the next phase, spanning days 21 through 30, focuses on actively cultivating positivity. The emphasis here is on proactive acts and behaviors that improve one's emotional and psychological well-being.

Practicing Gratitude

Gratitude is a profound and sincere appreciation for life's beautiful moments and characteristics. It's more than simply acknowledging pleasant occurrences or things; it's about feeling deeply grateful for them. Gratitude is more than a passing emotion; it is a way of being. Although the feeling of thankfulness originates within us, what we are often grateful for comes from sources other than ourselves, such as aid from family, the beauty of nature, or advice from a higher power. Embracing gratitude entails comprehending our interconnectivity and the external forces contributing to our well-being and happiness.

Individuals who frequently practice thankfulness report more positive feelings, a lower risk of depression, healthier relationships, and improved overall health.

Gratitude Journaling

A gratitude journal is one of the most effective methods to cultivate a mindset of gratitude. Gratitude journaling has become popular due to its profound effects on one's mind. The concept is simple: by maintaining a gratitude journal, you devote a small portion of your day to concentrate on the good things in your life consciously. Set aside a few moments each day to reflect on three to five things for which you are genuinely grateful. It could be as grand as a significant accomplishment or as simple as a stranger's smile or the flavor of your morning coffee. This simple act can significantly change your mental framework over time.

Writing accomplishes two things: For starters, it forces you to pause and concentrate on the positive aspects of your day, which may be especially helpful if you're going through a difficult time. It can help to balance out any unfavorable biases you may have naturally. Second, as you read through pages of positive comments over time, it serves as a reminder of the good in your life, essentially becoming a reservoir of positive memories. Furthermore, the act of journaling has therapeutic properties. Putting thoughts into words on paper helps clarify them. This positive activity encourages seeking and acknowledging the good, even when it may seem scarce. With practice, you'll notice that you begin to recognize moments of thankfulness throughout your day and build a more resilient and hopeful attitude in life.

Walks of Gratitude

Another powerful technique to cultivate thankfulness is to walk while reflecting on the many gifts in your life. It combines the advantages of light exercise with positive reflection. Focus on the sights, sounds, and sensations around you as you stroll in nature, your neighborhood, or your backyard. It could be birds singing, the scent of blooming flowers, the laughter of children playing nearby, or the sun's warmth on your skin. It may even be the crunch of falling leaves beneath your feet or the first frost on the trees around you. Grounding oneself in the present moment and savoring the simple pleasures stimulates a profound appreciation for the world around you. This technique might help you become more aware of the small blessings that frequently go unrecognized.

Participating in Enjoyable Events and Activities

Regularly seeking and participating in enjoyable activities is a guaranteed approach to improving one's happiness. Remember, the goal isn't to escape or avoid bad feelings but to gradually shift the balance in favor of positive emotions.

Here are some examples and ideas to get you started:

Nature walks: Going for a stroll in nature, whether it's a dense forest, a tranquil beach, or a peaceful park in your city, helps you to connect with the environment. The rustling of leaves or the sounds of ocean waves can instantly lift one's spirits.

Creative outlets: Activities such as painting, writing, or playing an instrument provide a sense of accomplishment and an opportunity for self-expression.

Learning anything new: Learning anything new, whether it's a culinary lesson, a dance workshop, or a foreign language, maybe invigorating. Celebrate minor victories along your learning path.

Volunteering: Lending a helpful hand without expecting anything in return can be extremely rewarding. Giving back can be fulfilling, whether at a local animal shelter, a community garden, or a nursing home.

Physical activity: Sports or a regular workout release endorphins, sometimes known as "happy hormones." Moving your body has definite sound effects on mood, whether dancing in your living room, cycling around your neighborhood, or taking a yoga session.

Travel: While this does not necessarily imply jetting off to a distant country (though why not if you can?), even weekend getaways or day journeys to see unfamiliar places can bring new insights and rejuvenate the mind.

Mindful moments: Activities such as meditation or simply sitting quietly with a cup of tea and focusing on the present moment can be incredibly refreshing.

Socializing: Spending meaningful time with loved ones, whether family or friends, frequently results in cherished memories. Organize a picnic or game night, or talk to someone you care about.

Attending workshops or seminars: Being surrounded by positive and like-minded people while learning about areas of interest can be enriching and inspiring.

Reading: Immerse yourself in an uplifting book, read inspiring biographies, or get lost in imaginary tales that take you to different realms.

You can develop a more optimistic outlook by intentionally capturing and relishing these moments. Recall that the objective is to arm oneself with a wealth of uplifting experiences and recollections, guaranteeing that the emotional balance is consistently tilted toward optimism and joy rather than avoiding adverse or challenging circumstances.

People ~ Places ~ Media: The Importance of Positive Surroundings

Our surroundings significantly impact how we think, act, and feel about ourselves. Humans are profoundly affected by their surroundings, much as plants are, needing the proper conditions of sunlight, water, and nutrition to flourish. Our interactions with others, the locations we visit, and the media we watch all impact us. To create an atmosphere that encourages positivity, development, and well-being, you must comprehend the importance of these three fundamental components: people, places, and media.

People: The Power of Company

A theory says we mirror the characteristics of the five closest individuals. These people affect our thoughts, behavior, habits, and even the goals we set for ourselves.

Positive Influences

Seeking out and cultivating relationships with positive people can have many advantages. Every interaction creates an impression on our minds. Positive people frequently exude contagious energy. Their positivity, perseverance, and can-do attitude can rub off on people around them, causing a chain reaction. When surrounded by such enthusiasm, one is likelier to adopt the same perspective, viewing obstacles as opportunities and defeats as lessons. Optimistic individuals are more than just cheerleaders; they frequently, although supportively, challenge us. They push us out of our comfort zones by asking the correct questions or providing an alternative viewpoint, thus encouraging discovery and improvements. They serve as mirrors, reflecting not just who we are but also the potential within us that we may ignore at times.

Positive people appreciate constructive feedback as much as they understand accomplishment. Their criticism isn't meant to bring you down but rather to assist you to rise higher. They respond to comments with empathy, ensuring the main point is received without undermining self-esteem. During chaotic times, their presence provides stability. Their ability to balance adversity offers comfort and a reminder that storms pass. With them by your side, obstacles appear manageable, and anxieties seem less intimidating.

These inspiring individuals frequently open our eyes to fresh viewpoints, concepts, and experiences. They assist in expanding horizons by sharing life lessons learned from their own experiences, suggesting a book that can change one's perspective, or introducing a new pastime. These new insights can spur personal growth by encouraging one to take previously unconsidered pathways.

Choosing a nutrient-rich diet for the soul is similar to surrounding yourself with positive people. The appropriate company nourishes the mind and spirit, keeping them resilient, upbeat, and agile, much as the proper nutrients nourish the body and keep it in shape.

Keeping Negative Interactions to a Minimum

It's essential to surround oneself with positive individuals, but it's also crucial to identify and avoid interacting with those who deplete energy or spread negativity. Rather than just severing relationships, it's necessary to understand and set boundaries and recognize limits to ensure that one's mental health is prioritized. Profoundly pessimistic people can unintentionally cloud your thinking, hinder your growth, and cause feelings of depression. Negative interactions can cause self-doubt, increased stress, and a warped sense of reality. Their doubts may eventually infiltrate your beliefs, causing you to view the world through a lens of limitations rather than possibilities. Adopting negative behaviors or attitudes, such as persistent whining, victimization, or believing that obstacles are insurmountable, is a risk.

Remember that everyone has bad days or goes through challenging situations. The issue emerges when negativity becomes a person's default mode of operation. Setting clear limits or allocating particular periods for interaction may be effective in these situations. It does not imply entirely cutting them out but ensuring your mental and emotional well-being is protected.

Positive Environments

Positive surroundings have a powerful psychological and physiological impact on people. The environments we live in have an enormous effect on our thoughts, feelings, and behaviors. Endorphins, serotonin, and dopamine, the neurotransmitters associated with happiness and contentment, can be stimulated in natural settings. Positive settings, such as social centers or group classes, enable people to interact with one another. Social connections are essential to the well-being of people because they provide emotional support, reduce feelings of loneliness, and develop a sense of belonging. Natural environments, such as beaches, forests, or lakes, offer a quiet environment that helps lower cortisol levels (the stress hormone) in the body. The soothing sounds of nature and visual beauty allow people to relax and rejuvenate.

Favorable Places to Visit:

1) **Nature Parks & Reserves**

   Spending time outdoors, breathing clean air, and savoring the peace can be incredibly therapeutic for the body and mind.

2) **Community Centers**

   These hubs are excellent places to meet new people, learn new skills, and participate in local events. They also provide a variety of activities.

3) **Libraries**

   Besides books, modern libraries frequently organize seminars, workshops, and group discussions that can be intellectually and socially stimulating.

4) **Museums and Art Galleries**

   Experiencing art and history may be a thought-provoking experience that inspires creativity and admiration.

5) **Yoga and Meditation Studios**

   These facilities provide a calm setting to practice mindfulness, flexibility, and mental peace.

6) **Cafés with a Positive Atmosphere**

   Some cafés, particularly those with wide spaces, plants, and soothing music, offer a relaxing environment to read, work, or reflect.

7) **Gardens and Botanical Spaces**

Being surrounded by plants and flowers, learning about their growth, and admiring their beauty can be therapeutic.

8) **Workshops and Classes**

Locations that offer classes in something new and intriguing, such as ceramics, painting, or learning a new language, can stimulate the brain and create a sense of accomplishment.

9) **Fitness Centers & Gyms**

Physical activity has been shown to improve mood. Endorphins, which are natural mood lifters, can be released during a successful workout.

10) **Venues for Live Acts**

Seeing live shows, whether theater, music, or dance, can be uplifting and provide a welcome break from the daily grind.

11) **Beaches and Lakeshores**

The sound of breaking waves or still water can be pretty peaceful, making beaches and lakes perfect for reflection and relaxation.

12) **Farmers' Markets**

These markets supply fresh produce and foster a sense of community. Getting to know local farmers and craftspeople can be a rewarding experience.

13) **Spiritual or Religious Centers**

These sites provide people solace, direction, and a stronger connection to their beliefs, creating inner calm.

14) **Volunteer Centers**

Contributing to a cause and helping others can bring tremendous purpose and happiness.

Book Clubs or Discussion Groups

Sharing opinions, debating ideas, and engaging in intellectual debates may be energizing and enlightening.

Spending time in these locations regularly can help break up the monotony of daily life by providing opportunities for personal growth, contemplation, and relationship building, all of which lead to a more positive mentality.

Choosing positive settings involves reducing exposure to hostile or poisonous environments. Limiting exposure to locations or events that encourage negativity, conflict, or excessive stress is just as important as seeking out pleasant spaces.

The Double-Edged Sword in the Media

Television, radio, print, and internet media all wield enormous power. It teaches, informs, entertains, and influences. Given its pervasiveness, it is critical to filter media consumption carefully.

Constructive Consumption

Consuming uplifting, instructive, and pleasant content can impact one's psyche. Inspirational podcasts, documentaries, and even light-hearted comedy can leave you feeling energized and knowledgeable.

Limiting Sensationalism

It is common knowledge that sensational news or dramatic content can cause stress, panic, or anxiety. While it is critical to keep informed, it is also vital to distinguish between helpful information and sensationalism. Choosing trustworthy news sources and minimizing exposure, especially during sensitive times, may help maintain mental balance.

Digital Detoxification

Digital devices are essential to our daily lives in today's interconnected world, providing convenience, connectivity, and entertainment. The steady influx of news, updates, and online dialogue can cause information overload, increasing tension and anxiety. Every notification ping, email alert, or social media feed scroll demands our cognitive attention. This constant mental strain can limit our capacity to focus, diminish memory recall, and influence our mood over time.

Frequent digital interruptions can disrupt our workplace and lengthen the time it takes to complete activities. Excessive screen use, particularly before night, has been linked to sleep disruption. The blue light emitted by digital devices disrupts the generation of melatonin, the hormone responsible for sleep regulation. Reduced nighttime screen time or regular digital detoxes can encourage improved sleep patterns, which boosts overall health.

A digital detox is a planned time away from screens, a modern solution to a problem. Periodic digital detoxes, even if they are brief, can boost productivity and provide the brain with much-needed rest, restoring cognitive function and improving concentration. A detox helps to remove oneself from potential digital pressures, making room for mental clarity and taking regular pauses from screens, whether phones, computers, or televisions. These detox periods are advantageous and require contemplation, connection with one's surroundings, and most importantly, a break from the constant assault of information.

With fewer digital distractions, our minds may roam, fantasize, and develop freely. This leisure may induce spurts of creativity, problem-solving, and contemplation, all of which are often suppressed by continual digital interaction.

Digital detoxes are about knowing when, why, and how we use our technology. We can manage the digital world balanced and health-consciously by taking regular breaks.

Chapter
4
INSTILLING POSITIVITY IN YOUR LIFESTYLE

Our daily routines and habits significantly impact how we feel about life and how healthy we are. Our ideas, feelings, and interactions are shaped by our decisions, which range from the habits we follow to the surroundings we design. As a result, incorporating positivity into our daily lives is imperative to living a happy, fulfilling, and purposeful life. Happy, contented, and fulfilled sensations become more consistent when positivity permeates all aspects of our lives. A good self-image and a positive lifestyle are frequently correlated. Maintaining positive surroundings and incorporating healthy practices strengthen our sense of self-worth. We start to believe that we are worthy people who can make wise decisions.

Thinking more openly and flexibly is associated with positivity. As a result, we may become more creative since we are more willing to consider fresh concepts and original solutions—a happier way of living results in a stronger sense of purpose.

Integrating optimism into every aspect of our lives goes beyond momentary joy. It's about creating a life focused on growth, development, fulfillment, and well-being despite ups and downs.

Positive Habits

Every day, as we deal with life's difficulties, we are led by habits and behaviors that are so normal that we hardly think about them. Whether apparent or not, these habits are critical in defining our mental health, clarity of mind, and general happiness. Having a cup of tea or coffee in the morning, going for a short walk in the evening, or meditating for a few minutes before bed are good habits and may seem insignificant initially. Still, these seemingly small acts we do repeatedly shape our more significant life stories. They shape our responses, feelings, and even our long-term goals, becoming the foundation of our daily lives. Our habits can either hold us back or help us shine. That's why it's essential to form good habits and routines.

Consider your everyday practices to be the foundation of your existence. Like a brick in a wall, each habit adds to the structure and solidity of your daily experience. Positive behaviors offer a solid basis for mental health and happiness. They serve as anchors, offering stability and regularity amid life's turbulence.

Negative habits, on the other hand, might operate as roadblocks, preventing us from realizing our greatest potential. They can cloud our judgment, dampen our mood, and distort our viewpoint, leading us away from the road of personal progress and fulfillment.

You can modify habits by selecting and developing beneficial behaviors that change your life story. Behaviors impact how we engage with others, influencing our relationships and social interactions. Positive habits can help us become more sympathetic, patient, and open to new experiences, which can improve our personal and professional relationships.

Developing and nurturing good habits is about enhancing certain aspects of our lives. It's about living a harmonious and fulfilling life.

Establishing Morning and Evening Habits That Encourage Positivity

How we begin each day profoundly affects our outlook and output for the rest of the day. Developing a regular morning routine that includes relaxing activities like meditation, writing in a diary, or doing a little workout can lay the groundwork for a positive and productive day. It's the promise one makes to oneself every morning that the day ahead will be abundant optimism.

The following are recommendations for morning and bedtime routines:

Morning: (when time is conducive to your schedule)

Physical Activity: Going for a brisk walk, doing some light yoga, or engaging in a more strenuous workout can elevate one's mood since it triggers the production of endorphins.

Breakfast: Fuel your body and mind with a wholesome breakfast or a protein-packed smoothie.

Stretching: A quick stretch in the morning helps stimulate blood flow, awaken the body, and make you feel more flexible and prepared for the day's activities.

Mindful Meditation: Start your day with ten to fifteen minutes of mindful meditation. Set a serene mood for the remainder of the day by paying attention to your breathing and clearing your thoughts.

Visualization: Take a few minutes to picture the day you have planned. Envision yourself accomplishing your chores with success and envision favorable results. Visualization helps to establish a constructive goal for the day.

Affirmation: Recite affirmations that are uplifting and that speak to you. These may include one's abilities, worth, or overall optimism. You are gradually altering your thought processes and increasing your self-assurance.

Tech-Free Time: Set aside 30 minutes in the morning without using electronics. You are spared from the instant barrage of emails, news, and social media updates, allowing you to begin your day with greater awareness.

Evening

Reflective Journaling: Write about your day in a journal for a few minutes. Focus on the day's positive experiences, lessons learned, and things you're grateful for.

Digital Detox: Set a specific time for putting away all electronic devices, ideally an hour or more before bedtime. Time away from electronics lowers your exposure to blue light, which might disrupt your sleep cycle.

Herbal Tea Ritual: Brew a cup of calming herbal tea, such as chamomile, to indicate to your body that it's time to unwind and prepare for sleep.

Reading: Instead of watching television, read a tangible book. Choose something light or uplifting to help you shift your thinking to a more serene state.

Mindfulness Meditation: Spend a few minutes in the evening focusing on deep breathing and releasing the day's worries.

Gratitude Exercise: Write down three things you were grateful for that day. Ending the day with thankfulness might help you feel better and sleep better.

Play Calming Music or Sounds: Make a playlist of soothing music or nature sounds. The quiet, peaceful background music can help you fall asleep faster and more deeply.

Physical Activity ~ Nutrition and Sleep: Keeping a Positive Outlook

Many people strive for a positive mindset by practicing meditation or positive thinking. However, our physical health, which involves exercise, proper nutrition, and adequate sleep, is vital for our mental wellness. These three factors are critical for overall well-being and have a major effect on how good we feel. Let's look at how each one contributes to positivity.

Physical Activity

Regular exercise promotes the release of endorphins, also known as 'feel-good' hormones. When endorphins are released, they help us feel happier and more relaxed by reducing pain and tension. Achieving fitness objectives or simply exercising can provide a sense of accomplishment. Self-esteem is increased and instills a positive attitude in other aspects of life. Exercise has been associated with enhanced cognitive performance, increased focus, and less mental tiredness. A clear mind is better able to think positively and solve problems.

Nutrition

Specific diets, such as those high in omega-3 fatty acids, antioxidants, and specific vitamins, help to regulate brain health and mood. Omega-3 fatty acids in seafood such as salmon can help with depression and mood swings. A healthy diet provides a continuous supply of glucose, the brain's principal energy source. Maintaining stable blood sugar levels can help to reduce mood swings and improve general cognitive function. Research indicates a strong link between gut health and brain function. Probiotics, fiber-rich foods, and a diet full of variety can boost gut health, which may impact brain function and mood. Reducing or eliminating the consumption of substances such as excessive caffeine, alcohol, and high-sugar foods can help to reduce mood swings and anxiety.

Sleep

Sleep is the therapeutic superpower and serves as a mental reset button. During deep sleep, the brain analyzes emotions and experiences, solidifies memories, and recovers. Adequate sleep guarantees that you wake up with a clear and new outlook. Sleep deprivation can cause irritation and emotional outbursts. Consistent sleep patterns assist with emotional regulation and stress management.

Sleep deprivation can interfere with concentration, decision-making, and creative thinking. A well-rested mind is more attentive, receptive, and optimistic. Physical healing is also boosted by adequate sleep. When the body feels well, the mind frequently follows.

Committing to regular physical activity, making smart food choices, and getting adequate rest benefits our physical and mental health.

The Positive Effects of Physical Spaces

Our moods and productivity levels are profoundly affected by the environments we spend time in. Be it our homes, workplaces, or leisure areas, the lighting, decor, and even the layout of any given space can enormously influence the mood of the occupants.

Our homes frequently reflect our inner states. They are more than just shelters; they are places where we can rest, renew, and find peace. Given how much time we spend indoors today, our homes must exude positivity and comfort.

Decluttering and Organizing Your Environment: Mental and Physical Advantages

Our surroundings, particularly our homes, mirror who we are. Physical clutter frequently reflects mental congestion. A cluttered environment may trigger emotions of overwhelm and tension. While a cluttered space may appear to be a minor issue, the repercussions of clutter are profound.

The atmosphere we create echoes our interior condition directly. Clutter can manifest procrastination, unsolved decisions, or even past traumas for specific individuals. A disorganized environment might unintentionally become a visual depiction of inner turmoil or anxiety.

According to research, congested surroundings may contribute to emotions of stress, fatigue, and sadness. When confronted with a cluttered environment, the brain becomes overstimulated, resulting in distractions and decreased focus.

A clean environment is not only appealing to the eyes; it also increases productivity. According to a Princeton University study, those who work in orderly spaces outperform those who operate in cluttered spaces. Tasks become more doable and time-efficient with fewer distractions and an organized structure in place.

Decluttering can be therapeutic. As you sort through your belongings, you are sifting through memories, decisions, and sentiments. Making decisions on what to keep and discard is a form of decision-making therapy. It aids in prioritizing, letting go, and gaining control of one's environment.

Donating is an integral part of decluttering. By donating items, you no longer need, you are making space in your home and helping the greater good. Knowing that your items may find a new purpose and bring joy to someone else might elicit sentiments of satisfaction and fulfillment. Sorting through your possessions and organizing items can provide tremendous relaxation and satisfaction.

On a symbolic level, decluttering signifies creating space for new experiences, memories, and opportunities. We communicate to ourselves and the universe that we're ready for growth and new beginnings by letting go of the old, tangible stuff or old behaviors.

A clutter-free bedroom can help you sleep better. Without distractions and a sense of order, the brain may relax, allowing for enhanced sleep. Furthermore, decluttered living areas encourage calmness, making reading or meditation more effective and enjoyable.

Decluttering is more than just an organizing effort; it is a psychological, emotional, and physical activity. By examining our spaces and possessions regularly and ensuring that everything has a place and a purpose, we are not only decluttering our surroundings but also laying the groundwork for mental clarity, increased productivity, and general well-being. In essence, decluttering is a form of self-care that allows personal development and a harmonious living environment.

Designing Spaces That Elevate Mood

Lighting

Lighting can significantly influence the way we feel. Serotonin, "the feel-good hormone," can increase levels with lots of light. Investing in high-quality, warm, adjustable lighting can be more enjoyable during the evenings. Try using salt lamps, candles, or fairy lights to give spaces a warm, inviting glow.

Color

Colors have psychological implications. Soft blues, for example, have a calming effect on the psyche, while warmer tones like orange and yellow can generate thoughts of warmth and happiness. Consider repainting walls or introducing new house furnishings in colors that correspond to the atmosphere you want to create. While individual reactions to color differ, pastel colors and earth tones are generally advised for creating a serene ambiance.

Earth tones are a color pallet influenced by nature that includes browns, tans, greens, and mellow yellows. They are frequently understated and can be warm or cool, linking inner rooms to the natural world outside.

Earth tones induce grounding, stability, and connectedness to the natural world. These hues may produce a relaxing, energizing atmosphere and a stable and reassuring presence. They're ideal for relaxation or concentration areas, such as living rooms or home offices.

A harmonious color palette creates an ambiance and is required to achieve a tranquil environment. Pastel and earth tones are used in various ways to produce a visually relaxing palette that appeals to the senses without being overbearing.

While keeping a large pastel or earth-toned palette, dashes of contrasting hues in the shape of accessories or furnishings may add life and keep the area from appearing dull.

Colors significantly affect our psychological and emotional states. Comprehending and utilizing the concepts of color psychology in our living areas can improve our daily lives by offering us a setting that is not only visually beautiful but also promotes mental and emotional health.

Beyond color, the texture and material of furnishings and decor profoundly affect the overall mood. Combining gentle colors with natural materials such as wood or stone may enhance a space's tranquility.

Sacred Areas

If feasible, set aside a space in your home for meditation, reading, or simply unwinding. This area should be free of electronic distractions. As the brain begins to associate this area with tranquility, simply entering it might induce emotions of relaxation and peace.

Décor

Integrating nature into our living environments can significantly impact our well-being. Houseplants, for example, enhance air quality and add life and vibrancy. A NASA study even revealed the air-purifying qualities of particular houseplants, resulting in a healthier living environment. Small indoor water elements like fountains can introduce running water's peaceful and meditative sounds.

Introduce items with personal importance or that generate happy memories. Include photographs, travel souvenirs, or even artwork. Surrounding yourself with items that hold personal meaning can serve as daily reminders of joyful memories and treasured experiences.

Chapter

5

BEYOND 30 DAYS: SUSTAINING POSITIVITY

A 30-day positivity challenge is a great way to get started, but true transformation takes more time than that. It takes consistent work to keep a positive frame of mind. Your mind must constantly be nourished and fed positive stimuli to remain optimistic. It entails continuously exposing yourself to places, people, and circumstances that encourage positive thinking. Your dedication to personal development ensures you will have a more remarkable ability to bounce back from the inevitable setbacks that life brings.

Our brains typically tend to focus on the negative, a survival instinct inherited from our ancestors, who were constantly alert for predators. Without conscious effort, we may be drawn to negativity. We may combat this inherent predisposition and create a mental environment where positivity can thrive by engaging in actions that elevate our spirits and sharpen our focus regularly.

How to Handle Obstacles and Setbacks

Setbacks and obstacles are an unavoidable part of life. No path is ever perfectly smooth, and it is often during difficult times that we learn the most important lessons and receive the most significant insights. How we respond to these challenges is imperative.

Acceptance

First and foremost, acknowledge the situation. It will not go away if you deny or ignore it. Acceptance does not imply agreement with what occurred but rather an acknowledgment of the reality of the situation.

Reframe Your Perspective

While you may not always be able to influence what happens to you, you can always control how you see it. Every problem should have a positive aspect or a lesson. This mental adjustment can turn a setback into an opportunity for growth.

Remember to Breathe

Stay grounded. A few deep breaths can help reduce the immediate emotional response, allowing you to examine the situation more objectively.

Seek Help

Speak with someone you trust. Simply expressing your concerns and fears might be helpful at times. Furthermore, a new viewpoint may provide solutions or insights you had yet to consider previously.

Break It Down

If the activity appears overwhelming, divide it into smaller, more achievable tasks or steps. Challenges will seem more manageable and provide a clear path forward.

Action Over Contemplation

Overthinking can paralyze you. Choose action over contemplation. Instead, concentrate on concrete steps you can take. Even minor activities can build momentum and help you feel more in control.

Maintain Consistency

Maintaining consistency can be grounding in the face of upheaval. While breaking away from habits or routines may be tempting, they can act as anchors, providing a sense of normalcy.

Self-Compassion

Be kind to yourself. Keep in mind that everyone makes mistakes and endures difficulties. What distinguishes us is not the lack of setbacks but how we respond to them.

Limit Unpleasant Input

While staying informed is crucial, continual exposure to unwelcomed news or pessimistic people can increase emotions of negativity. Selectively allow what (and who) into your mental space.

Examine and Reflect

Take some time to reflect when the storm has passed. What did you discover? How can you improve your preparation for the next time? These insights can be helpful in future issues.

Even though obstacles and setbacks can be intimidating, they also offer opportunities. We can withstand these challenges and often become more assertive and wiser by persevering, looking for growth in adversity, and arming ourselves with the necessary resources. It's not about avoiding the storm but learning to dance in the rain.

Continual Practices: Meditation ~ Journaling ~ Affirmations

Consistency is essential for deeply ingraining any practice into one's lifestyle. These three activities, in particular, are transforming for many people.

Meditation

Meditation can help to relax the mind, reduce stress, and promote mindfulness over time. It is not about silence but about acknowledging your thoughts without judgment. Maintaining a consistent meditation program may serve as a stabilizing force amidst chaos as life evolves.

Journaling

Journaling is an exemplary tool for processing emotions, reflecting on events, and setting intentions. Regular journaling lets you track your growth, recognize repeating trends, and appreciate small, everyday pleasures.

Affirmations

Affirmations reinforce positive attitudes about oneself and the world. You may fight and manage negative thoughts and self-sabotage by repeating affirmations daily. Positive affirmations can transform your views, leading to a more optimistic and robust mindset.

Creating the Ideal Environment

Your environment can have a significant effect on how you feel. It's imperative to create an atmosphere that encourages positivity.

Personal Spaces

- Organize your home and office.

- Get rid of any clutter.

- Fill them with things that make you feel good.

- Good lighting, plants and colors that make you feel relaxed can all improve the overall mood.

Set Limits

It's vital to set limits for yourself, both mentally and physically. It could mean eliminating waste, selecting precise work hours, or limiting personal relationships. In personal interactions, boundaries are like invisible lines that tell others how we want to be treated and what we expect from them. They protect our mental and emotional health and help us connect with others in a healthy way.

Before you can create boundaries, you must first determine what you are and are not comfortable with. Consider previous circumstances in which you felt taken advantage of, disrespected, or overwhelmed. Recognizing these feelings can help you figure out where to draw the line. Once you've established your boundaries, be sure you convey them effectively. Avoid using confusing statements. Instead, be precise about your requirements and expectations. There must be more than merely establishing a limit once. It is critical to maintain consistency in reinforcing it. If you've communicated a specific boundary, keep to it, even if it's complicated. This consistency communicates the importance of the boundary to others over time. While establishing your boundaries is critical, respecting those of others is also vital. Remember that setting limits does not imply being rigid or pushing others away. It's all about putting your mental and emotional well-being first. This joint approach promotes mutual understanding and respect, resulting in healthier relationships.

Building Positive Connections

Relationships are what make life worth living. The way we feel about these individuals affects not only our emotional health but also our mental and physical health in significant ways. The kind of relationships we have can either make our lives better or make us unhappy and stressed. Being around people who make you feel good can make a huge difference. Having a few deep, meaningful ties is better than having a lot of superficial relationships.

Prioritize genuine connections and encourage open dialogue. Deal with problems head-on and share your happiness.

Reduce Negativity: Media ~ Gossip ~ Toxic Environments

We are inundated with interactions and information in our daily lives that can influence our mood, thoughts, and general well-being. The constant barrage of sensational news stories and rumors can be exhausting. Because of this, it's important to be aware of how negativity might enter through different doors. Here's a closer look at three crucial areas where negativity frequently appears and how to manage them.

Negative Media Consumption

From upsetting news articles to jealously inspiring social media posts, news and entertainment may frequently be sources of negativity. Relentless exposure to unfavorable media can cause anxiety, pessimism, and warped perceptions of reality.

The things we read and watch can have a significant effect on how we feel and what we think. However, a steady flow of toxic media can have harmful effects:

News Outlets: Sensationalist and disturbing news items, frequently focusing on conflict, tragedy, or scandal, can dominate our news feeds.

Social media platforms, whether in the form of controversial viewpoints, aggressive ideas, or polarizing news, can be filled with posts that cause jealousy, inadequacy, or discontent.

Movies, TV shows, and online entertainment may spread negativity through violent, upsetting, or dystopian themes.

Psychological and Emotional Effects

Persistent exposure to unpleasant news or social media can heighten emotions of anxiety, and stress leading to a constant state of concern or fear.

Pessimism and an Unpleasant Outlook

Consistently consuming distasteful content can affect your impression of the world, resulting in a generally pessimistic outlook and a depressed mood. Excessive consumption of negative media can distort your vision, causing you to believe the world is more brutal, dangerous, or hopeless than it truly is.

Social Comparison and Jealousy

As users compare their lives to the frequently idealized images and narratives others give, social media, in particular, can elicit feelings of inadequacy or envy.

Desensitization to Violence

Exposure to violent or disturbing content regularly can lead to desensitization, making you less compassionate or more accepting of such reality.

Media Consumption Management

1. Select news sources that report fairly and avoid sensationalism. Limit your time on social media and be informed about the accounts you follow.

2. Approach media with skepticism. Question the sources, comprehend the potential biases, and detect the attention-grabbing strategies.

3. Seek out media that uplifts, educates, or positively engages you. This can include inspirational stories, instructive content, or enjoyable or relaxing entertainment.

4. Set aside specific periods for media consumption and stick to them to avoid media consumption becoming an all-consuming hobby.

Consider how media consumption influences your emotions and thoughts regularly. Mindfulness activities can assist in maintaining a balanced viewpoint.

Gossip

The act of spreading information about people who are not present during a conversation, typically of a personal or private nature, is known as gossip. It usually entails discussing facts, rumors, or assumptions about another individual's life, conduct, or private matters.

Rumors frequently disseminate information that is either false or untrue. It may entail fabricating information, or disclosing private information without authorization. Rumors and incomplete information may follow a gossip victim into their personal and professional life, causing irreversible harm to their reputation.

Being the target of rumors can cause tension, worry, and a sense of being teased or alone in society. It can also give the gossiper a false sense of power or superiority.

Gossiping or being around gossip may be detrimental to relationships. It can also create a poisonous atmosphere that increases tension and mistrust. Gossip may occasionally give rise to legal issues, mainly when it involves disclosing confidential information or acts of libel or slander.

Talking or listening to gossip can occasionally serve as a social bonding mechanism, making people feel more connected to one another. But this camaraderie is frequently superficial and might encourage a distrusting environment.

People can use gossip as a tool to exert control or domination over others in society. Gesturing false information about others allows gossipers to influence opinions or social structures within a group.

Gossip can contribute to a toxic environment in social groups or the workplace by making people uncomfortable or hesitant to share, preventing sincere communication and collaboration.

Even while it could appear like a typical, innocent pastime, gossip can have adverse effects that are severe and long-lasting. Understanding gossip for what it is and making a deliberate effort to avoid it may lead to stronger, more authentic, and trusting relationships. Focusing on polite, honest, and open communication creates a good and encouraging atmosphere for all.

Management Tips:

Refrain from participation: Make a conscious decision to refrain from engaging in rumors or disparaging remarks about other people.

Modify the Topic: Shift the conversation's focus to more uplifting or productive subjects.

Think About the Impact: Examine the effects that gossiping has on your relationships and emotions.

Toxic Environments

Mental health can be significantly impacted by being in an unhealthy or hostile environment, whether it be at work, home, in a group, or in social gatherings. Chronic stress, low self-esteem, and even depression can result from it. If an environment consistently brings you down or triggers negative emotions, it might be time to re-evaluate your association.

It is crucial to understand that pursuing positivity is a constant process, not a final state of perfection. It all comes down to making decisions that resonate with your desired life and mindset. You'll be resilient enough to face life's obstacles if you put in the effort, surround yourself with supportive individuals, and develop self-awareness.

Tips for Management:

Establish Boundaries: Tell people clearly and concisely what actions you will and won't tolerate.

Seek Support: Discuss your struggles with dependable family members, friends, or professionals.

Think About Modifications: Sometimes, leaving a consistently harmful atmosphere may be the wisest action.

Create a Supportive Network: Spend time with individuals who make you feel good, encourage you, and provide value to your life.

Controlling negative information from the media, rumors, and unhealthy surroundings is critical to preserving mental and emotional health. Although many things are outside our control, we still have power over our responses to them and the decisions we make to safeguard our well-being.

The Next Steps:

Customizing the Positivity Practice for Sustainability

Like any other aspect of self-improvement, the key to sustaining a positive mindset is ensuring it can be maintained over time.

Here are some ways to keep your focus on the positive:

Self-evaluation

Take a step back occasionally to examine what is and isn't working.

Remember that what worked for you initially may need to be tweaked as you grow and expand.

Flexibility

Positivity is not a one-size-fits-all concept. Modify or try something different if a given practice feels too challenging or doesn't resonate with you.

Integrate Positivity Practices into Daily Life

Instead of viewing positivity practices as a separate chore, consider how you might organically include them in your daily routine. You can, for example, listen to uplifting podcasts or say affirmations while driving.

Keep up to Date

New methods, strategies, and tools related to positive psychology will emerge as knowledge and research advances. Keep up with the latest information to ensure your practice remains relevant and practical.

Workshops

Workshops are instrumental because they frequently offer a more hands-on and participatory experience, which is beneficial. Look for any local seminars or workshops dealing with positivity or related subjects. Participating in activities with people with similar interests can also provide support, encouragement, and new points of view.

CONCLUSION

Now that you've concluded this guide, take a moment to pause and think about the journey you've been on over the past month. This journey into the domain of positivity was about changing your thinking and life.

Every action, every exercise, and every pause for contemplation has been a vital component in constructing a better and more upbeat outlook for the foreseeable future. The 30-day structured program may have sparked change, but the only way to experience lasting transformation is to make these practices an intrinsic part of your routine.

Remember that the pursuit of optimism is a journey, not a goal in and of itself. Although the last month may have presented some difficulties and prompted some moments of uncertainty, the persistent work, the daily decisions, and the steadfast devotion will shape this journey into a lifetime of satisfaction and contentment.

In light of this, remember to keep the flame of positivity alive as you move forward. Accept the techniques as they are, modify them as you gain more experience, and make continuous efforts to improve yourself. Remember to share what you've learned with others as you start to feel the positive effects of this life-changing adventure. We want to hear about your experiences, the obstacles you overcame, the triumphs you celebrated, and the lessons you learned. Please feel free to share them with us. Your experience has the potential to serve as a ray of sunshine for someone else, illuminating their way toward positivity.

In this vast adventure called life, packed with a wide range of experiences and feelings, let the positivity you feel guide your steps. Continue to encourage others, have an optimistic outlook, and be a source of light.

APPENDICES

Recommended Readings

Norman Vincent Peale: "The Power of Positive Thinking"

Shawn Achor: "The Happiness Advantage"

Carol S. Dweck: "Mindset: The New Psychology of Success"

James Clear: "Atomic Habits: An Easy & Proven Way to Build Good Habits and Break Bad Ones"

The Dalai Lama and Howard Cutler: "The Art of Happiness"

Online Resources Promoting Positive Thinking

https://www.centreofexcellence.com

http://positivityhub.net

Additional Journaling Prompts

Make a list of five things that made you smile today.

How do you define happiness in your life?

Recall a difficult situation and how you overcame it.

What are the three most important lessons you've learned this month?

How would your life change if you let go of something that is now holding you back?

Describe a time when you were incredibly proud of yourself.

What are three qualities you admire in others and want to develop in yourself?

Write about a compliment that you will never forget.

Consider the positive influences in your life and how they shaped you.

Collection of Affirmations

"I am deserving of joy, love, and peace."

"Every challenge I face is an opportunity for growth."

"I am constantly evolving and bettering myself."

"I radiate positivity and attract goodness into my life."

"My past does not define me; it prepares me."

"I am in charge of my happiness and well-being."

"Every day I am becoming more resilient and confident."

"I am deserving of every compliment I receive."

"The strength within me is greater than any obstacle before me."

"I choose to fill my mind with positive and nourishing thoughts."

ABOUT THE AUTHOR

Bonnie is a strong supporter of positive living. She embarked on a journey to learn more about the transformational power of positive thinking, motivated by personal experiences and a desire to help others overcome emotional hurdles. This investigation created "The Negative Thought Detox: 30 Days to Positivity," a book intended to help people break free from the shackles of negativity and enjoy a life filled with joy, resilience, and peace.

Bonnie delivers practical, easy-to-follow ways to build a happy mindset with a compassionate approach and an in-depth understanding of the obstacles faced by people battling negative thoughts. Her book is not only a reflection of her desire to assist others in finding inner peace, but it is also a testimony to the belief that happiness is achievable by anyone. Bonnie's goal with this book is to encourage readers to alter their lives, free themselves from stress and worry, and begin a journey to long-term happiness and fulfillment.

www.ingramcontent.com/pod-product-compliance
Lightning Source LLC
Chambersburg PA
CBHW061302120726

48001CB00001B/447